MW00966984

The Estate Planning Today Handbook

By Louis S. Shuntich, J.D., LL.M.

All the best,
Lou Shuntich

MARKETPLACE BOOKS
Columbia, MD

This Book Is Dedicated:

To my mother Sarah for all the times she hurt her
hands working so that I could be a lawyer.
And to my father Louis for all the times he had to
remind me that he was my father, and not my
friend but was the best friend I ever had.

Copyright © 2003. Louis S. Shuntich.
Published by Marketplace Books, Inc.

All rights reserved.

Reproduction or translation of any part of this work beyond that permitted by Section 107 or 108 of the 1976 United States Copyright Act without the permission of the copyright owner is unlawful. Requests for permission or further information should be addressed to the Permissions Department at Traders' Library.

This publication is designed to provide accurate and authoritative information in regard to the subject matter covered. It is sold with the understanding that neither the author nor the publisher is engaged in rendering legal, accounting, or other professional service. If legal advice or other expert assistance is required, the services of a competent professional person should be sought.

From a Declaration of Principles jointly adopted by a Committee of the American Bar Association and a Committee of Publishers.

> This book, along with other books, are available at discounts that make it realistic to provide them as gifts to your customers, clients and staff. For more information on these long-lasting, cost-effective premiums, please call John Boyer at 800-272-2855 or e-mail him at john@traderslibrary.com.

ISBN 1-59280-060-2

Printed in the United States of America

Contents

Foreword

Acommitment to lifelong learning was one of the fundamental principles upon which the Society of Financial Service Professionals was founded back in 1928. While our industry, our culture, our society has changed significantly in the intervening 75 years, this basic tenet has never wavered.

The Society distinguishes itself among other financial service membership organizations with its requirement that members hold a recognized degree or credential, such as CLU, CFP, CPA, JD, ChFC, and CEBS. The Society's goal is to create a professional home for these credentialed individuals who share a belief in a core set of values—education, ethics, and relationships.

The Society of Financial Service Professionals's goal is to create a professional home for credentialed individuals who share a belief in a core set of values — education, ethics, and relationships.

As the professional home for our members, the Society provides a vibrant environment for professional growth and the tools to support such growth, such as a Code of Professional Responsibility, access to networking opportunities, and continuing education programs and services.

The Society's mission statement highlights a commitment to continuing education that is current, comprehensive, and practical, and which extends the collective wisdom of our membership. We feel confident that you will find *The Estate Planning Today*

Handbook informative, interesting, and useful. And we wish you happy and fulfilling travels in your journey of professional learning.

Sincerely,

Alan R. Ziegler, CEBS, CLU, ChFC
President, *Society of Financial Service Professionals*

Introduction

According to a Cornell University study, the baby boomers will inherit eight trillion dollars from their parents. This will represent the greatest transfer of wealth in the history of our nation. Consequently, it will require tremendous amounts of life insurance, financial products and professional services to minimize and pay transfer taxes while meeting other estate-planning objectives. To take full advantage of this opportunity, as a provider of those products and services, you will have to be knowledgeable about estate planning and be able to identify each client's unique estate-planning needs.

To that end, this book contains a conceptual explanation of estate planning that will enable you to see the forest in spite of the trees. In addition, you will be taught how to think like an estate planner so that you can apply the step-by-step process of analysis that will enable you to identify your client's needs, and match them to the appropriate solutions within your discipline. Put simply, you will first be taught what can be done, and then, how to figure out *what* to do.

Since any kind of professional endeavor is a lifelong learning process, there is certainly more to know about estate planning than is contained in this book. In addition, regulations change frequently and advisors must consult a variety of sources to stay in step with the latest modifications. However, this book will enhance your basic understanding and act as a logical and initial framework to which your additional knowledge can attach in a meaningful way.

CHAPTER 1

Technical Overview of Estate, Gift and Generation-Skipping Taxes

What Is Estate Planning?

Estate planning is a problem-solving process that allows an individual to build, conserve and transfer their estate to subsequent generations at the lowest tax cost possible, while also taking care of their own lifetime needs. You should notice two points about this definition. First, it is a problem-solving process that enables individuals to identify and reach their goals. Second, it covers all phases of their life, from estate building in the early years to estate conservation and distribution at death. In that regard, the focus of this book is on the later period of life in terms of explaining what can be done to minimize transfer taxes while taking care of the person's lifetime needs and providing a plan for the distribution of their assets upon death, with sufficient funds to pay any remaining estate tax.

Estate planning is a problem solving process that allows an individual to build, conserve and transfer their estate to subsequent generations at the lowest tax cost possible, while also taking care of their own lifetime needs.

To assist clients in accomplishing these goals you need to develop enough familiarity with the transfer tax rules to be able to recognize estate-planning problems and their related solutions. The transfer tax provisions referred to are the federal estate, gift and generation-skipping (GST) tax laws. (Although not covered in this book, the effect of corresponding state transfer-tax laws should also be considered in any given case.) Accordingly, the purpose of this chapter will be to give you an overview of the federal transfer-tax laws, which will enable you to understand the planning opportunities that are explained in subsequent chapters.

Overview of the Economic Growth and Tax Relief Reconciliation Act of 2001

Essentially, the Economic Growth and Tax Relief Reconciliation Act of 2001 (hereinafter referred to as the 2001 Tax Act) provides only modest transfer-tax relief and does not fundamentally alter the transfer-tax structure. Further, the changes take effect in three phases. In the first period, from 2002 through 2009, there are both gradual reductions in the maximum transfer-tax rates and increases in the amount of property that is exempt from transfer tax. Then in phase two, for the year of 2010 only, the estate and generation-skipping taxes are repealed, a carryover basis system replaces the current step up in basis for property received from a decedent, and the gift tax applies at a maximum marginal rate of 35%. Finally, in phase three, unless there is further legislative action, the law as it existed in 2001 will be reinstated on January 1, 2011. This means that if Congress does not take any more action on these issues, there will only be a one-year window, during 2010, when there will be a gift tax but no estate and generation-skipping taxes.

Carryover Basis

Under the current system, when a person dies their heirs inherit the decedent's property at a tax basis equal to the fair market value of the property at the decedent's death. This is called a "step up in basis," since the value of property frequently appreciates between the time a decedent acquires it and dies. The step up benefits the heirs for income-tax purposes if the property has appreciated in the hands of the decedent. This is because the heirs may sell it using the fair market at the decedent's death as their income-tax basis, rather than the lower figure that the decedent paid for the property.

The 2001 Tax Act replaces the step-up-in-basis approach with a carryover basis system that applies for the one year that the estate tax is repealed. Under the carryover approach, the decedent's heirs take as their basis the lesser of the decedent's adjusted basis (generally the cost of what the decedent paid for the property) or the fair market value of the property at the date of the decedent's death. In addition, each decedent is allowed a limited $1.3 million step up that is allocated to specific items of the decedents property by the decedent's executor. Finally, a further $3 million of step up may be added to the basis of property that passes to the decedent's spouse and qualifies for the estate-tax marital deduction (explained below).

Impact of the 1976 Tax Reform Act

Prior to 1976, the gift and estate-tax rates were separate, with the gift-tax rates being lower to encourage the transfer of property through our society. The 1976 Tax Reform Act, however, created a unified transfer-tax system under which the estate and gift-tax rates were combined into a single table of graduated rates, that, prior to the 2001 Tax Act, ranged from 18% to 55% as follows:

The 2001 Tax Act replaces the step-up-in-basis approach with a carryover basis system that applies for the one year that the estate tax is repealed. Under the carryover approach, the decedent's heirs take as their basis the lesser of the decedent's adjusted basis (generally the cost of what the decedent paid for the property) or the fair-market value of the property at the date of the decedent's death.

Amount of Transfer		Rate of Tax	
Over —	*But not over —*		*of the excess amount over —*
		. . . . 18%	$0
		$1,800 plus 20%	$10,000
		$3,800 plus 22%	$20,000
		$8,200 plus 24%	$40,000
		$13,000 plus 26%	$60,000
		$18,200 plus 28%	$80,000
		$23,800 plus 30%	$100,000
		$38,800 plus 32%	$150,000
		$70,800 plus 34%	$250,000
		$155,800 plus 37%	$500,000
		$248,300 plus 39%	$750,000
		$345,800 plus 41%	$1,000,000
		$448,300 plus 43%	$1,250,000
		$555,800 plus 45%	$1,500,000
		$780,800 plus 49%	$2,000,000
		$1,025,800 plus 53%	$2,500,000
		$1,290,800 plus 55%	$3,000,000

The effect of the progressive rates in the unified table was strengthened by the requirement that an individual's tax liability be calculated on the basis of their cumulative transfers over their lifetime and at their death. This works to raise taxes because counting prior transfers under an increasing rate structure tends to push a taxpayer into higher marginal brackets with each additional transfer.

The 2001 Tax Act modified the above table by reducing the maximum estate and gift-tax rates as follows:

Calendar Year	Highest Estate & Gift Tax Rates	Calendar Year	Highest Estate & Gift Tax Rates
2002	*50%*	*2007*	*45%*
2003	*49%*	*2008*	*45%*
2004	*48%*	*2009*	*45%*
2005	*47%*	*2010*	*35% gift tax only*
2006	*46%*		

Accordingly the estate and gift tax tables for the years 2002 through 2004 will be as follows:

Estate and Gift Tax Table Year 2002

Amount of Transfer		Rate of Tax	
Over —	*But not over—*		*of the excess amount over—*
$0	$10,000	. . . . 18%	$0
$10,000	$20,000	$1,800, plus 20%	$10,000
$20,000	$40,000	$3,800, plus 22%	$20,000
$40,000	$60,000	$8,200, plus 24%	$40,000
$60,000	$80,000	$13,000, plus 26%	$60,000
$80,000	$100,000	$18,200, plus 28%	$80,000
$100,000	$150,000	$23,800, plus 30%	$100,000
$150,000	$250,000	$38,800, plus 32%	$150,000
$250,000	$500,000	$70,800, plus 34%	$250,000
$500,000	$750,000	$155,800, plus 37%	$500,000
$750,000	$1,000,000	$248,300, plus 39%	$750,000
$1,000,000	$1,250,000	$345,800, plus 41%	$1,000,000
$1,250,000	$1,500,000	$448,300, plus 43%	$1,250,000
$1,500,000	$2,000,000	$555,800, plus 45%	$1,500,000
$2,000,000	$2,500,000	$780,800, plus 49%	$2,000,000
$2,500,000	. . . .	**$1,025,800, plus 50%**	**$2,500,000**

Estate and Gift Tax Table Year 2003

Amount of Transfer		Rate of Tax	
Over —	*But not over—*		*of the excess amount over—*
$0	$10,000	. . . . 18%	$0
$10,000	$20,000	$1,800, plus 20%	$10,000
$20,000	$40,000	$3,800, plus 22%	$20,000
$40,000	$60,000	$8,200, plus 24%	$40,000
$60,000	$80,000	$13,000, plus 26%	$60,000
$80,000	$100,000	$18,200, plus 28%	$80,000
$100,000	$150,000	$23,800, plus 30%	$100,000
$150,000	$250,000	$38,800, plus 32%	$150,000
$250,000	$500,000	$70,800, plus 34%	$250,000
$500,000	$750,000	$155,800, plus 37%	$500,000
$750,000	$1,000,000	$248,300, plus 39%	$750,000
$1,000,000	$1,250,000	$345,800, plus 41%	$1,000,000
$1,250,000	$1,500,000	$448,300, plus 43%	$1,250,000
$1,500,000	$2,000,000	$555,800, plus 45%	$1,500,000
$2,000,000	. . . .	**$780,800, plus 49%**	**$2,000,000**

Estate and Gift Tax Table Year 2004

Amount of Transfer		Rate of Tax	
Over —	But not over—		of the excess amount over—
$0	$10,000	. . . . 18%	$0
$10,000	$20,000	$1,800, plus 20%	$10,000
$20,000	$40,000	$3,800, plus 22%	$20,000
$40,000	$60,000	$8,200, plus 24%	$40,000
$60,000	$80,000	$13,000, plus 26%	$60,000
$80,000	$100,000	$18,200, plus 28%	$80,000
$100,000	$150,000	$23,800, plus 30%	$100,000
$150,000	$250,000	$38,800, plus 32%	$150,000
$250,000	$500,000	$70,800, plus 34%	$250,000
$500,000	$750,000	$155,800, plus 37%	$500,000
$750,000	$1,000,000	$248,300, plus 39%	$750,000
$1,000,000	$1,250,000	$345,800, plus 41%	$1,000,000
$1,250,000	$1,500,000	$448,300, plus 43%	$1,250,000
1,500,000	$2,000,000	$555,800, plus 45%	$1,500,000
$2,000,000	. . . .	**$780,800, plus 48%**	**$2,000,000**

As previously stated, after 2004 the last highest bracket will continue to change each year until 2009, after which the estate tax is repealed for 2010 and the gift-tax rates will be as shown below.

Unified Credit/Exemption Equivalent

The 1976 Tax Reform Act also created the concept of a unified credit, under which taxpayers were granted a tax credit of $192,800 against taxes stemming from their cumulative dispositions of property. Prior to 1998, that credit translated into an individual's ability to transfer over life, at death, or in combination of both, up to $600,000 of property, tax free. (This $600,000 figure is referred to as the exemption equivalent.)

By applying the exemption equivalent to the previous table for years prior to 2002, you can see that the tax rates actually began at 37% since cumulative transfers of less than $600,000 were exempt. Further, the benefit of the lower rates and the exemption equivalent were phased out on cumulative transfers of between $10,000,000 and $21,040,000. That was accomplished through the imposition of an additional 5% surtax on such intermediate transfers. This resembled the phase-out of the personal exemption, and itemized deductions, that occurs under the federal income tax, for individuals with income above certain limits. In this regard, the Taxpayer Relief Act of 1997 eliminated the phase-out of the unified credit starting in 1998, and the 2001 Tax Act eliminated the phase-out of the lower rates starting in 2002. In addition, pursuant to the Taxpayer Relief Act of 1997, the unified credit and the exemption equivalent were to be gradually increased for gifts made or individuals dying after 1997. (The actual terms used to describe the unified credit and exemption equivalent in the 1997 act are the "applicable credit amount" and the "applicable exclusion amount" respectively.)

The increases in the applicable credit amount and applicable exclusion amount under the Taxpayer Relief Act of 1997 were as follows for the years 1997 through 2001:

Year	Applicable Credit Amount	Applicable Exclusion Amount
1997	$192,800	$600,000
1998	$202,050	$625,000
1999	$211,300	$650,000
2000-2001	$220,550	$675,000

Subsequently, the 2001 Tax Act effectively separated, and then further increased, the applicable exclusions for the gift and estate taxes as follows:

The actual terms used to describe the unified credit and exemption equivalent in the 1997 act are the "applicable credit amount" and the "applicable exclusion amount" respectively.

		Gift Tax Applicable Exclusion	Estate Tax Applicable Exclusion
	Year		
	2002	$1,000,000	$1,000,000
	2003	$1,000,000	$1,000,000
	2004	$1,000,000	$1,500,000
	2005	$1,000,000	$1,500,000
	2006	$1,000,000	$2,000,000
	2007	$1,000,000	$2,000,000
	2008	$1,000,000	$2,000,000
	2009	$1,000,000	$3,500,000
	2010	$1,000,000	Estate Tax Repealed
	2011	$1,000,000	$1,000,000

(Note that this means starting in 2004 the estate and gift tax exclusions are no longer truly unified since the amounts are different.)

The Estate Tax

Generally within nine months after an individual's death, a federal estate-tax return (Form 706) must be filed, if the size of their estate exceeds their estate-tax applicable exclusion amount. The calculation of the tax, which is usually payable with the return, involves five steps. The steps are described below, and to help you keep track of the overall picture, a conceptual summary follows the explanation.

STEP 1 — Gross Estate

The computation of a decedent's estate-tax liability begins with the determination of their gross estate. This is comprised of the fair market value of all the property in which they have an interest at their death. For this purpose, what a decedent has an interest in includes what they own completely, as well as the following categories of partial ownership:

- Property the decedent has previously transferred and either kept an interest in for the rest of their life, or retained the right to determine who will enjoy it.

- Property the decedent has transferred and over which the decedent has retained a reversionary interest. (The right to get the property back under certain conditions.)

- Property which the decedent has transferred but retained the right to change who will enjoy it.

- Life insurance paid to the decedent's estate or in which the decedent possessed incidents of ownership. (Ownership rights such as the right to name a beneficiary, take policy loans, etc.)

- Property over which the decedent has a general power of appointment. (The power to direct that the property be given to themselves, their estate, or the creditors of their estate.)

- The present value of annuities or similar payments receivable by a person after surviving the decedent, if the decedent had the right to receive payments under the same contract during their life.

- Property in which the decedent had a joint interest with another person and the other person acquires full ownership of the property by reason of surviving the decedent. (The general rule is that the entire value of the property is included in the decedent's estate, except to the extent that the other person can show that they contributed to its cost. In the case of married couples, however, where both spouses are U. S. citizens only one-half of the property's value is included in the decedent's estate, regardless of who provided the purchase price.)

- Property in which the decedent was left a life income interest by their previously deceased spouse that was excluded from the spouse's

Generally within nine months after an individual's death, a federal estate-tax return (Form 706) must be filed, if the size of their estate exceeds their estate-tax applicable exclusion amount. The calculation of the tax, which is usually payable with the return, involves five steps:
1. **Gross Estate**
2. **Adjusted Gross Estate**
3. **Taxable Estate**
4. **Federal Estate Tax Before Credits**
5. **Net Federal Estate Tax**

estate. (This is called qualified terminable interest property and will be explained later.)

- Life insurance in which the decedent has given away incidents of ownership within three years of death. In addition, where the decedent has given away property interests like those described in the first three points above, within three years of their death, the value of such property is also included in the decedent's estate.

STEP 2 — Adjusted Gross Estate

The next step is the calculation of the adjusted gross estate which is arrived at by deducting from the gross estate funeral and administrative expenses, debts, casualty and theft losses. (As will be explained later, this figure is significant to the determination of the estate's ability to qualify for the special provision permitting the installment payment of any estate-tax liability over 15 years, as opposed to the normal nine months.)

STEP 3 — Taxable Estate

After determining the decedent's adjusted gross estate, that figure is reduced by the marital deduction, and the charitable deduction, to reach the taxable estate.

After determining the decedent's adjusted gross estate, that figure is reduced by the marital deduction, and the charitable deduction, to reach the taxable estate.

The marital deduction is equal to all the property which passes to the decedent's spouse in certain prescribed ways. This includes what goes to the spouse outright, as well as that which the spouse receives in trust. Where a trust is utilized the spouse must be entitled to all the trust income, and be given the right to say who gets the remainder of the trust property after the spouse's death. Alternatively, in the case of what is called a QTIP trust, the spouse is given all the income but no control over who receives the remainder. This provision was designed for individuals in second marriages who have children from their first marriage. It enables them to take care of the second spouse while assuring that the children of their first marriage will receive their inheritance.

The objective of the marital deduction is to delay the taxation of such property until after the surviving spouse's death. This permits the surviving spouse to have the benefit of such property, unreduced by tax, for the remainder of his or her life. Note however, that any such property remaining at the surviving spouse's death will be exposed to estate tax in the spouse's estate upon his or her death.

Property which the decedent leaves to charity is included in the gross estate but is also deducted in arriving at the taxable estate. (The reason is to encourage charitable giving.)

STEP 4—Federal Estate Tax Before Credits

This figure is calculated by adding to the taxable estate the amount of any adjusted taxable gifts which are comprised of the taxable part of gifts made by the decedent since 1976. (The purpose here is to give effect to the unified concept of the transfer tax structure by calculating the estate tax on the basis of cumulative transfers during life and at death.) This total, called the tentative tax base, is then applied to the unified rate schedule to calculate the tentative tax.

Finally, using the unified tax rate in effect at the decedent's death, the amount that would have been paid on the decedent's post-1976 gifts is figured and

The objective of the marital deduction is to delay the taxation of such property until after the surviving spouse's death. This permits the surviving spouse to have the benefit of such property, unreduced by tax, for the remainder of his or her life.

deducted from the tentative tax to arrive at the estate tax payable before credits. (The reason for deducting the tax on post-1976 gifts is to avoid double taxation of those transfers, since they were already subject to tax at an earlier stage of the calculation as a part of the tentative tax base.)

The federal estate tax, before credits, is reduced by applicable, state, foreign, and prior transfer credit.s to arrive at the net federal estate tax.

STEP 5 — Net Federal Estate Tax

The federal estate tax, before credits, is reduced by the following credits to arrive at the net federal estate tax:

- **Applicable credit** — The purpose of this credit is to eliminate estates of modest size from the transfer tax structure. *(Note that the amount of the credit and corresponding exemption will be gradually increasing during the period from 2002 through 2009.)*

- **State death tax** — This figure gives the estate a limited offset for death taxes paid at the state level. *(Pursuant to the 2001 Tax Act, the state death-tax credit is reduced by 25% in 2002, by 50% in 2003, by 75% in 2004 and repealed in 2005. In 2005, and thereafter, it is replaced with a deduction.)*

- **Foreign death taxes** — Like the credit for state death taxes this item provides an offset for foreign death taxes.

- **Prior transfers** — Under certain circumstances an estate is given a credit for tax paid on property that was previously included and taxed in someone else's estate.

Conceptual Summary

The above steps may be briefly described as follows:

Gross estate	Total of decedent's property interests
Less	Estate expenses, debts thefts and losses
Equals	Adjusted gross estate
Less	Marital and charitable deductions
Equals	Taxable estate
Plus	Adjusted taxable gifts
Equals	Tentative tax base
Times	Unified tax rate
Equals	Tentative tax
Less	Unified tax on post-1976 gifts
Equals	Estate tax payable before credits
Less	Applicable, state, foreign & prior transfer credits
Equals	Estate tax payable

It should be noted that for the one year (2010) that the estate tax is repealed, under the 2001 Tax Act, estate tax returns will be required to be filed for "large transfers." Essentially, this includes any transfer of property (except cash) that has a value in excess of $1.3 million. The information to be required on the "Section 6018 Return" includes a description of the property, tax basis, holding period and fair market value. Further, within 30 days of filing the information with the IRS, it must be provided to the beneficiary(s) receiving the property from the decedent.

The Gift Tax

This is a tax imposed on the value of property that an individual transfers, by gift, during their lifetime. The value used for purposes of calculating the tax is the "fair market value" of the property on the date of the gift. The donor who makes the gift is the party responsible for filing a gift tax return (Form 709), which is normally due by April 15th of the year following the year in which the gift is made. Payment of any tax that is due must usually be made with the return. If the tax is not paid by the donor, the donee is liable for the tax, up to the value of the gift.

The tax is applied to the gifts that an individual makes during each calendar year, after the subtraction of certain exclusions and deductions. As previously explained, the tax is calculated on a cumulative basis whereby the gifts of prior years are counted in determining the tax on the current year's transfers. This means that the prior year's gifts tend to drive the current year's gifts into higher marginal tax brackets. The exclusions and deductions allowed in figuring the tax are as follows:

The tax is applied to the gifts that an individual makes during each calendar year, after the subtraction of certain exclusions and deductions:
- **Annual Exclusion**
- **Exclusion for Qualified Transfers**
- **Marital Deduction**
- **Charitable Deduction**

- **Annual Exclusion**

  The "annual exclusion" is an aspect of the gift-tax law that allows individuals to give as many people as they want $11,000 per year, gift-tax free, without the need to file a gift-tax return. Consequently, if an individual had three children, he or she could give each child $11,000 per year, or a total of $33,000 annually. In addition, if the individual is married, and their spouse chooses to join them in making the gifts, the couple can give up to $22,000 per year to as many people as they please, even though all the funds come from just one of the couple. (This is called gift splitting and requires the filing of a gift-tax return.) For example, a husband and wife with three children could give each child $22,000 per year, for a total of $66,000 annually. (Note that pursuant to the Taxpayer Relief Act of 1997, the annual exclusion is indexed for inflation after 1998 and the $11,000 figure is the amount of the gift-tax annual exclusion as adjusted for inflation in 2002. The indexing is to be rounded down to the next lowest multiple of $1,000. This means that it will be some years before the annual exclusion can be expected to increase again, due to the current low inflation rates.)

- **Exclusion for Qualified Transfers**
  There is no gift tax on amounts paid on behalf of an individual to an educational organization for their instruction, or to a provider of medical care for their treatment.

- **Marital Deduction**
  Just as the estate-tax marital deduction exempts certain transfers, at death, to a surviving spouse, from the estate tax, the gift-tax marital deduction exempts similar lifetime transfers to a spouse from the gift tax. This includes outright transfers to the spouse, as well as those in trust where the spouse has the right to all the income from the property and the power to direct the disposition of the remaining principal after his or her death. In addition, QTIP-type trusts qualify where the spouse is given the right to trust income, but the donor spouse directs who is to receive the remainder after the donee spouse's death.

- **Charitable Deduction**
  There is a deduction from the gift tax for gifts to charity. Where the gift is in the form of an income interest, or a remainder interest in property, as will be explained later, there are specific rules that must be followed for the deduction to apply.

Calculation of the Gift Tax for Years Until 2009

The subtraction of the above exclusions and deductions from the fair market value of an individual's transfers during a year results in the determination of the person's "taxable gifts" for that year. A tax on the year's taxable gifts until 2009 is then calculated in the three following steps:

STEP 1—Using the unified tax rate, calculate the tax on the total of the current year's and all prior year's taxable gifts.

STEP 2 — Applying the unified rate, compute the tax on just the prior years' taxable gifts.

STEP 3 — Subtract the amount of tax determined under STEP 2 from that figured under STEP 1. The difference is the gift tax on the current year's taxable gifts.

The current year's gift tax is offset against the donor's remaining applicable credit amount. It should be noted that this offset is not optional. Rather, it is automatic and will reduce the amount of the credit that is available to offset the tax on future gift transfers, or the amount of any estate tax that may be due at the donor's death. Further, if the amount of tax on the donor's lifetime transfers exceeds the amount of his or her applicable gift-tax credit, a tax will be payable to the extent of the excess during the donor's life. (Utilizing the concept of the applicable gift-tax exclusion, instead of the applicable gift-tax credit, another way of saying this is that an individual can make up to $1,000,000 of taxable gifts in between 2002 and 2009 without having to pay a gift tax.)

Calculation of the Gift Tax After 2009

For years after 2009, the gift-tax rate schedule will be as follows:

Amount of Transfer		Tentative Tax	
Over —	But not over —		of the excess amount over —
$0	$10,000	. . . . 18%	$0
$10,000	$20,000	$1,800, plus 20%	$10,000
$20,000	$40,000	$3,800, plus 22%	$20,000
$40,000	$60,000	$8,200, plus 24%	$40,000
$60,000	$80,000	$13,000, plus 26%	$60,000
$80,000	$100,000	$18,200, plus 28%	$80,000
$100,000	$150,000	$23,800, plus 30%	$100,000
$150,000	$250,000	$38,800, plus 32%	$150,000
$250,000	$500,000	$70,800, plus 34%	$250,000
$500,000	. . . .	$155,800, plus 35%	$500,000

The steps for calculating the gift tax on gifts for 2010, using the above schedule, is as follows:

STEP 1 — Using the above tentative tax schedule, calculate a tax on the current year and all prior years' taxable gifts.

STEP 2 — Using the above tentative tax schedule, calculate a tax on just the prior year's taxable gifts.

STEP 3 — Subtract the amount of tax determined under STEP 2 from that figured under STEP 1. The difference is the gift tax on the current year's taxable gifts for 2010.

Generation-Skipping Tax

The best way to approach an explanation of the Generation-Skipping Tax (GST) is to provide an understanding of why the tax was enacted. To do that, an example of the kind of planning that took place before the passage of the law is helpful. In that regard, individuals who were seeking to avoid the estate tax used to place property in trust with the provision that the income from the property was to be paid to their children, with the remainder passing to their grandchildren after the childrens' deaths. The reason for this tactic was to provide for the children, and then the grandchildren, without having the trust property subject to estate tax at the childrens' deaths. This strategy worked because the estate tax is only imposed on property that individuals own at their deaths, and the children would not be deemed to own the property at their deaths. The reason is that they only had the right to income from it during their lives, and no interest in it after their deaths. Essentially, this meant that by taking such an

Generation-Skipping Tax is a federal tax that is imposed on transfers to individuals who are two or more generations below that of the grantor. Its purpose is to prevent the avoidance of tax on a generation through the mechanism of a donor making transfers that skip over the generation in question.

approach, individuals could "skip" paying transfer tax for a family "generation" while still giving that generation the benefit of the property. Consequently, it led to the passage of the current version of Generation-Skipping tax law, in 1986, to prevent such tax-avoidance techniques from working.

A skip person is someone who belongs to a generation that is two or more generational levels below that of the transferor.

The way the GST operates to fill in the gap left by the estate tax is to impose a tax when there is a transfer of property to an individual described as a "skip person." A skip person is someone who belongs to a generation that is two or more generational levels below that of the transferor. This is deemed to occur on three specific events that are described in the law. They are a "direct skip," a "taxable termination" and a "taxable distribution." A definition of each of those terms, with an example of how they operate, is as follows.

Direct Skip

A "direct skip" is a transfer to a skip person that is subject to estate or gift tax.

Example: A grandparent makes an outright gift of $100,000 to a grandchild. This is a direct skip because it is subject to gift tax and is a transfer to a skip person (grandchild) who is two generations below the transferor (grandparent). In this respect, it should be noted that transfers to a grandchild are not considered a direct skip if the grandchild's parent is deceased. This rule, called the "predeceased parent exception," was extended by the 1997 act to cover transfers to grandnieces and grandnephews, occurring after 1997, when the decedent has no living lineal (direct) descendants.

There are certain exemptions from the rule on direct skips. These include payments to a person or institution that are for the donee's medical treatment, or education, and gifts that qualify for the annual gift-tax exclusion. Regarding annual exclusion gifts that are made to a trust, the exemption from GST does not apply unless two additional requirements are met. They are that no one else can receive any part of the beneficiary's gift during their life, and the gift will be included in the beneficiary's estate if the beneficiary dies before the trust terminates.

The taxable amount of a direct skip is the amount received by the transferee. Liability for the tax rests with the transferor, except where the gift is in trust, in which case the trustee is responsible for the tax.

Taxable Termination

A "taxable termination" occurs under a trust when the interests of non-skip persons terminate and only skip persons are left as beneficiaries of the trust.

Example: A parent establishes a trust for their child and three grandchildren. Upon the child's death the only trust beneficiaries remaining are the grandchildren. This is a taxable termination because upon the death of the child (non-skip person) only the grandchildren (skip persons) are left as trust beneficiaries. It should be noted that the 1997 act extended the predeceased-parent exception to taxable terminations if the parent of the beneficiary in question was dead at the time the transfer first becomes subject to estate or gift tax.

There is an exception to the definition of taxable termination for payments covering the tuition or

A "taxable termination" occurs under a trust when the interests of non-skip persons terminate and only skip persons are left as beneficiaries of the trust.

medical expenses of a skip person. Otherwise, the amount of any property subject to the termination is the amount exposed to taxation and the trustee is liable for the tax.

Taxable Distribution

Taxable Distribution is a payment of income or principal from a trust to a person who is a skip person.

This is a payment of income or principal from a trust to a person who is a skip person.

Example: An individual establishes a trust for their child and grandchild. Subsequently, while the child is still alive, the trust makes a payment to the grandchild. This is a taxable distribution because it involves a payment from the trust to the grandchild, who is a skip person.

Further, as previously mentioned with regard to taxable terminations, the 1997 act also extended the predeceased-parent exception to taxable distributions, when the parent is deceased at the time that the transfer first becomes subject to estate or gift tax.

Payments from the trust to cover the medical or educational expenses of the skip person are not considered taxable distributions. The rest of what is paid to the distributee is subject to tax, which is owed by the distributee.

GST Exemption

Every person has a "Generation-Skipping Tax Exemption," which they may use to reduce or eliminate the tax on their transfers of property. (The original $1 million exemption is indexed for inflation after 1998, and rounded to the next lowest multiple of $10,000 in accordance with the 1997 act. However, for 2003 the exemption is increased to $1,120,000.) It will continue to be indexed through 2003 after which it will be equal to the estate-tax exemption equivalent as follows:

Year	GST Exemption
2004	$1.5 million
2005	$1.5 million
2006	$2 million
2007	$2 million
2008	$2 million
2009	$3.5 million
2010	GST repealed

Note that pursuant to the 2001 Tax Act, the GST will be repealed for the year 2010, only, after which current law will again apply.

This is similar to the operation of the applicable exclusion amounts for purposes of the estate and gift-tax laws. Like the applicable exclusions, the GST exemption can be allocated over life and/or at death to the individual's cumulative transfers. The GST exemption may be allocated by an individual, or their executor, to any transfer of property with respect to which the individual is deemed to be the transferor. Generally, this can be one at any time from the day of the transfer until the time for filing the individual's estate-tax return, including extensions.

Automatic Allocation of GST Exemption to Indirect Skips

Prior to the 2001 Tax Act, the GST exemption was automatically applied to direct skips but not to indirect skips. In that regard, an "indirect skip" is any transfer of property to a generation-skipping tax

Every person has a "Generation-Skipping Tax Exemption," which they may use to reduce or eliminate the tax on their transfers of property.

trust that is not a direct skip, and is subject to the gift tax. For this purpose a "generation-skipping tax trust" is a trust that meets the following three requirements:

- The trust could have a taxable termination or taxable distribution with respect to the transferor.

- Under the terms of the trust it is unlikely that more than 25% of the trust corpus will be subject to tax in the estate of a non-skip person, such as the transferor's child.

- The trust is not one of certain types of charitable lead or charitable remainder trusts.

To apply the exemption to indirect skips (or not have it apply to direct skips) an election had to be made by filing a gift-tax return. If that election was made on a timely filed gift-tax return, it was effective from the date of the transfer. Alternatively, if an untimely return was used to make the election, it was effective from the date of the return. The effective date of the election can be very important when it is being applied to appreciating property (like investments or life insurance). The reason is that the earlier the exemption is applied to property that is increasing in value, the less of the exemption it takes to cover the value of the property. (Put simply, more property value uses up more GST exemption.) This made the election procedure a trap for the unwary. Consequently, the 2001 Tax Act sought to remedy this situation by providing that, for transfers after December 31, 2000, the transferor's unused GST exemption will be automatically allocated to indirect skips made during the transferor's life (unless the transferor elects out of such allocation).

The effective date of the election can be very important when it is being applied to appreciating property — like investments or life insurance. The reason is that the earlier the exemption is applied to property that is increasing in value, the less of the exemption it takes to cover the value of the property.

In this regard, the automatic allocation was not intended to apply to those situations where such an allocation would be undesirable. (Cases where it is unlikely that a generation-skipping transfer would take place, and it would probably be a waste of the transferor's GST exemption to allow it to be automatically applied.) Specifically, because of the definition of a GST trust, the automatic allocation does not apply to:

- Transfers to a trust where, by the terms of the trust, it is likely that more than 25% of the trust corpus will be taxed in the estate of a non-skip person such as the transferor's child.

- Transfers to certain charitable lead and charitable remainder trusts.

Unfortunately, until further guidance is given, it seems unsafe to rely upon the exceptions to automatic allocation, where the transferor's spouse is a beneficiary of the trust. For example, the exceptions do not seem to cover the common situation of a discretionary trust for the benefit of the spouse, and children, that will terminate in favor of the children at stated ages after the spouse's death. This means that it will be necessary to examine each case in light of the specific exceptions to the automatic allocation rule to make sure that it is not being applied when proper planning would dictate against it. Further, when one of the exceptions would not cover an undesirable automatic allocation, the transferor will have to consider making an election against automatic allocation by filing a gift-tax return. Such returns are due by April 15th of the year following the calendar of the transfer.

Retroactive Allocations of the GST Exemption

The 2001 Tax Act provided further relief by permitting retroactive allocations of the GST exemption to situations where a taxable termination occurs because of a death "out of order." This change was made to cover those situations where a transferor did not allocate GST exemption to a trust, because the trust was

The 2001 Tax Act provided further relief by permitting retroactive allocations of the GST exemption to situations where a taxable termination occurs because of a death "out of order."

expected to only benefit non-skip persons such as children of the transferor. In some situations, however, the non-skip person may die prematurely and upset the transferor's plans. This would occur, for example, where a child of the transferor unexpectedly dies and causes the trust to terminate (taxable termination) in favor of the transferor's grandchild. To remedy this situation, the 2001 Tax Act permits the GST exemption to be retroactively allocated, using the value of the property on the date it was transferred to the trust. This provision applies to the deaths of non-skip persons occurring after December 31, 2000. Consequently, it could be helpful to transferors who made transfers in trust before 2001 and chose not to allocate their GST exemption, but experience a death out of order after December 31, 2000. Note that, as previously stated, for transfers after 2000, the transferor is generally covered by the automatic allocation of the GST exemption for direct and indirect transfers. In that regard, the new provision could also be helpful to transferors who elect out of the automatic allocation, and subsequently experience a death out of order. In any case, the retroactive allocation must be made on a gift-tax return filed by April 15 of the year after the calendar year in which the non-skip person died.

Calculating the Generation-Skipping Tax

The actual tax rate applied to a transfer of property is a product of the highest federal estate-tax rate (50% in 2002 and dropping to 45% by 2009), multiplied by the "inclusion ratio." This inclusion ratio is 1 minus the "applicable fraction." The numerator of the applicable fraction is the amount of GST exemption allocated to the transferred property, and the denominator is the value of the transferred property less certain deductions. The deductions are the amount of federal or state estate tax, paid by any trust holding such property, as well as any estate or gift-tax charitable deductions allowed with respect to such property. Accordingly, the applicable fraction appears as follows:

GST Exemption Allocated to Property

Value of property less death taxes and charitable deductions

Example: A grandfather transfers $2 million in trust for his grandchild in 2004 and his $1.5 million GST exemption is automatically allocated to the transfer. Assuming there are no deductions or exemptions, the applicable fraction is $1,500,000/$2,000,000 or .75. Further, the inclusion ratio is 1 - .75 (or .25). Consequently, since the maximum estate tax rate for 2004 will be 48%, the GST rate on the transfer is .25 X 48% or 12%. Accordingly, the tax on the transfer is 12% X $2,000,000 or $240,000.

CHAPTER 2

Estate-Tax Savings Techniques That Do Not Involve Gifting

No Universal Solution

There is no panacea for solving the estate-tax concerns of all individuals. Rather, what we have are a variety of techniques for dealing with their differing situations. The question of whether any particular approach is available for a client's use depends upon the specific facts of the case, and beyond that, the willingness of the person to do what is required to take advantage of the opportunity. In this regard, you will find that at times an individual can be made aware of an opportunity but, for personal reasons, they will not utilize it. You should not allow this to frustrate you. The reason is that estate planning is a highly personal matter, and what any individual ultimately chooses to do with their property will be decided by their values, and not yours. Your responsibility is to make them aware of their options, and then, within the limits of your profession, help them to carry out what they choose to do without being judgmental.

Estate planning is a highly personal matter and what any individual ultimately chooses to do with their property will be decided by their values and not yours. Your responsibility is to make them aware of their options.

Another fundamental point is that estate planning is not just focused on saving taxes. Rather, the principal concern is with helping people take care of themselves and their families in accordance with their set of values. With proper planning, however, those personal objectives should be accomplished at the lowest tax cost possible. Consequently, the balance of this chapter will be devoted to discussing certain "basic" estate-tax savings techniques that may be considered as a starting point. This is because of their relatively broad applicability, and the fact that they do not require the making of gifts, which involves a higher threshold of commitment by the individual. After these techniques are exhausted, virtually all other approaches to saving estate taxes dictate that the person make gifts. Since the gifting route to estate-tax savings also offers great opportunities, those techniques will be covered in later chapters.

Our review of the non-gift approaches to estate-tax savings begins with an explanation of why people need a will and then covers how that document can be drafted to minimize estate taxes.

Our review of the non-gift approaches to estate-tax savings begins with an explanation of why people need a will and then covers how that document can be drafted to minimize estate taxes. Subsequently, we shall examine a provision that allows the estate tax value, and, consequently, the estate-tax liability, to be lowered for certain real estate used in farming or for a small business. Then we will cover a provision of the 1998 act that allows an executor to elect to deduct up to a certain amount of a decedent's "family-owned business interests" from his or her taxable estate. Finally, we shall consider the requirements of a provision that permits certain estate-tax liabilities to be paid in installments at a favorable rate of interest.

The Will as the Basic Estate-Planning Document

Generally, all estate planning should start with a person's will. This is because if a person dies intestate (without a will) state law dictates who gets that person's property that could have passed by will. This type of property, called "probate property," does not include certain kinds of assets that are jointly held (such as a home or a bank account) with a right of "survivorship," or assets that pass by a contractual beneficiary designation (such as life insurance or qualified pension benefits). The undesirable consequences of having the property pass by state law are that the people who get the property, and the portions they receive, may not be in accordance with what the decedent would have wanted. (Typically, one-third to one-half goes to the decedent's spouse and the balance to their children.) Further, if property passes to a minor, a person the decedent did not like, or trust, might be made the guardian of the property for the child.

It should be noted that where a married couple holds their major assets jointly, with right of survivorship, there may be very little property that passes under the will of the first person to die. The reason, as previously stated, is that the jointly held property, with right of survivorship, does not constitute probate property, and therefore, does not pass under the first decedent's will. Rather, because of the survivorship aspect of its ownership, it passes automatically to the remaining spouse. It is upon that second person's death that the will becomes critically important, however, since the property is no longer jointly held and the survivor's will controls its disposition.

The undesirable consequences of having the property pass by state law are that the people who get the property, and the portions they receive, may not be in accordance with what the decedent would have wanted.

If a married couple or any other joint owners of property do not want their interests to pass automatically to the survivor, they may hold their ownership interests as "tenants in common," rather than as "joint tenants with right of survivorship." Where the property is held as tenants in common, each party has the ability to pass their interest to whom they please according to the terms of their will. Alternatively, if they have no will, it passes under the terms of their state's intestacy law.

Drafting the Will to Minimize Estate Taxes

Besides the non-tax reasons why a person should have a will, there is also the fact that the will is usually the starting point in any planning to minimize federal estate taxes.

Besides the non-tax reasons why a person should have a will, there is also the fact that the will is usually the starting point in any planning to minimize federal estate taxes. This is because, as shall be explained, it is generally through their will that married individuals take advantage of the marital deduction and their unified credits to transfer up to $2,000,000, in 2002, and up to $7,000,000, by 2009, to their children estate-tax free. (Remember, however, that the estate tax is repealed for the year 2010, and then automatically returns in 2011 to the law as it was prior to the 2001 Tax Act. This means that the estate-tax applicable exclusion will return to $1,000,000 on January 1, 2011, unless there is further legislative action.)

The unlimited federal estate-tax marital deduction dates from 1981 and, as indicated in Chapter 1, provides that all the property that an individual leaves to their surviving spouse passes free of federal estate tax. Taken at first blush, this seems to suggest that all an individual has to do to save estate tax is leave all their property to their spouse at their death. While it is true that this avoids estate tax at the first death, it could be a mistake, because it might cause an unnecessary increase in estate tax at the surviving spouse's death. The reason is that the first spouse to die would not be properly utilizing their applicable estate-tax credit (applicable estate-tax exclusion ranging from $1,000,000, in 2002, to $3,500,000 by 2009).

Generally, the ideal approach from an estate-tax perspective is to direct, in the individual's will, that an amount equal to the applicable estate-tax exclusion be placed into a "by-pass" trust, with the remainder of the estate being given to their surviving spouse under the marital deduction. This will avoid any estate tax at the first death, because an amount equal to the exclusion is shielded by the applicable estate-tax credit, while the balance of the estate is covered by the marital deduction. A logical question at this point, however, is whether the spouse should object to an amount equal to the exclusion being placed in the by-pass trust rather than being given to him or her. The answer is that the spouse need not be concerned, since the will can provide that all the income from the amount in the by-pass trust must be given to the spouse, plus as much of the principal as the trustee thinks appropriate. In addition, the trust can state that the spouse has the right to demand the greater of $5,000, or 5%, of the trust corpus (principal) each year. Consequently, while the spouse does not own the property in the trust, it is all available for the spouse's benefit.

Generally, the ideal approach from an estate-tax perspective is to direct, in the individual's will, that an amount equal to the applicable estate-tax exclusion be placed into a "by-pass" trust, with the remainder of the estate being given to their surviving spouse under the marital deduction.

The significant advantage of the by-pass trust/ marital deduction approach becomes apparent when the surviving spouse dies. This is because the value of the property in the by-pass trust will not be included in the spouse's estate, and therefore, will not be subject to federal estate tax. The reason is that the spouse will not be deemed to own the property in the trust, and the estate tax only applies to property that the decedent owns at death. That is true regardless of what has happened to the value of the property in the by-pass trust during the surviving spouse's life. This means that even if the property in the trust has appreciated during the spouse's life to more than the original amount placed in the trust, the full value will still be excluded from the spouse's estate, and be exempt from federal estate tax.

The amount that is taxed at the surviving spouse's death will be what is left of what the spouse received under the marital deduction, which when added to the spouse's own separate property exceeds the amount of the spouse's estate-tax applicable exclusion. The benefit of using the by-pass trust, in combination with the marital deduction, as opposed to giving all the property to the surviving spouse under the marital deduction, is illustrated by the following example: Assume that the first spouse dies in 2002 (when the applicable exclusion is $1,000,000) with an estate of $3,000,000 and the surviving spouse who dies in 2004 (when the applicable exclusion is $1,500,000) has nothing. Note that, for purposes of this calculation, the applicable exclusion is used instead of the applicable credit, but the results are identical.

Unlimited Marital Deduction	Marital Deduction in Excess of Applicable Credit
First Death in 2002	*First Death in 2002*
$3,000,000 Gross Estate $3,000,000 Marital Deduction $0 Taxable Estate	$3,000,000 Gross Estate $2,000,000 Marital Ded/$1,000,000 By-Pass $0 Taxable Estate
Second Death in 2004	*Second Death in 2004*
$3,000,000 Gross Estate $1,500,000 Applicable Exemption $1,500,000 Taxable Estate $705,000 Tax	$2,000,000 Gross Estate $1,500,000 Applicable Exemption $500,000 Taxable Estate $225,000 Tax

As can be seen from this example, $480,000 can be saved by simply dividing the estate between the marital deduction and a by-pass trust. One caution should be kept in mind, however, and that is that if the surviving spouse in the above example had died first, their applicable estate-tax exclusion would have been wasted. This is because that spouse had no separate property, of his or her own, with which to set up a by-pass trust in the event they die first. What this suggests for tax planning, is that the spouse with the $3,000,000 should consider giving an amount equal to the applicable estate-tax exclusion to the spouse with no property. That would enable the less wealthy spouse to utilize their applicable estate-tax credit to set up a by-pass trust. This would guarantee the same overall tax savings, whichever spouse died first. (You should note that because of the unlimited gift-tax marital deduction, there is no gift tax on transfers between spouses to accomplish this objective.)

Non-U.S. Citizen Spouse

Generally, the marital deduction is not available unless the decedent's surviving spouse is a U.S. citizen. In this regard, if a surviving spouse receives property that does not qualify for the marital deduction because they are not a U.S. citizen, the problem can be solved by having them become a U.S. citizen. This must be done, however, before the date for filing the decedent's estate-tax return, and the surviving spouse must remain as a resident of the U.S. between the date of the decedent's death and becoming a citizen.

If the surviving spouse will not become a U.S. citizen, the unlimited marital deduction will not be

Generally, the marital deduction is not available unless the decedent's surviving spouse is a U.S. citizen.

available unless the property is placed in a Qualified Domestic Trust or "QDOT." To be effective, such a trust must have at least one trustee who is an individual U.S. citizen, or a domestic corporation, and the trust must elect to be treated as a QDOT. Further, such a trust can take the form of any trust that would qualify for the unlimited marital deduction, except that there is no requirement for distributing all current income to the surviving spouse. Finally, an estate tax is imposed on distributions of principal from the trust, unless the distributions are because of a "hardship" situation.

If a U.S. citizen dies without creation a QDOT, it can be set up by their surviving non-citizen spouse. The conditions are that the surviving spouse can only use property that passes to them outright, and the trust must be established before the date for filing the decedent's estate-tax return.

The 2001 Tax Act repeals, in 2010, the estate tax imposed on the value of property remaining in a qualified domestic trust at the death of the non-citizen surviving-spouse beneficiary. The 2001 Tax Act, however, retains through December 31, 2020, the estate tax on lifetime distributions to a surviving spouse from a QDOT created by a decedent dying before 2010.

For planning purposes, it should also be noted that while there is no unlimited gift-tax marital deduction for gifts by a U.S. citizen to their non-citizen spouse, such a spouse may be given a gift, tax-free ($112,000 for 2003, as adjusted for inflation).

Bracket Shifting

Since the federal estate brackets will range from 18% to 45% through 2009, it may be advisable to consider taking advantage of the bracket differences by not fully utilizing the marital deduction, and paying some estate tax at the first death. For example, assuming that an individual has an estate of $6,000,000, and their spouse has no assets, the tax savings may be demonstrated as follows:

Individual defers all estate tax until second death through utilization of the by-pass trust and marital deduction.

Tax at individual's death in 2002	$ 0
Tax at surviving spouse's death in 2004	$1,665,000
Total tax after both deaths	$1,665,000

Individual leaves ½ of estate or $3,000,000 in a trust that is taxable to the extent that it exceeds the individual's applicable exclusion amount of $1,500,000 in 2004.

Tax at individual's death in 2002	$925,000
Tax at spouse's death in 2004	$705,000
Total tax after both deaths	$1,230,000

The tax savings of $435,000 is accomplished by exposing some of the individual's estate to tax on the first death, at lower tax brackets. This works by avoiding the lumping of the individual's entire estate into the higher brackets under the progressive structure of the estate tax. It should be noted that the savings would be smaller to the extent that the individual's estate is less than $6,000,000.

Since the federal estate brackets will range from 18% to 45% through 2009, it may be advisable to consider taking advantage of the bracket differences by not fully utilizing the marital deduction, and paying some estate tax at the first death.

Special Use Valuation of Farm or Small-Business Property

In 1976, Congress enacted Internal Revenue Code section 2032A, finding it desirable to encourage the continued use of real estate for farming and other small-business purposes. Prior to the passage of section 2032A, real estate that was included in a decedent's estate was valued at its fair market value. Consequently, where the realty was used for farming or other small-business purposes, including it in the estate at fair market value often created a substantially higher estate-tax liability than was warranted, considering the value of its use as a farm or small-business operation.

Section 2032A permits real estate that qualifies to be valued in the estate on the basis of its actual use, rather than its higher fair market value. This means that where the provision applies, it grants relief to the heirs of farmers and small-business owners who wish to carry on the family business, and might otherwise find that fair market value produces such a large estate tax that they have to sell the property to pay the tax.

Section 2032A permits real estate that qualifies to be valued in the estate on the basis of its actual use, rather than its higher fair market value. The problem with section 2032A, however, like other tax-saving provisions, is that it requires certain conditions to be met.

There is an $840,000 limit, per decedent, as of 2003, on how much real estate may be reduced from i ts fair-market value to its actual use value. For example, assume that the estate of a decedent contains qualifying farmland with a fair market value of $1,400,000 that is worth $400,000 as a farm. It will be included in the estate at a value of $560,000. This is because while the difference in value is $1,000,000, the maximum reduction is only $840,000. Here it should be noted that between a husband and wife the total reduction in value after both deaths is two times $840,000, or $1,680,000. Further, for estates of decedents dying after 1998, the 1997 act indexes the original $750,000 limit for inflation (rounded to the next lowest multiple of $10,000). Consequently, as of 2003 the limit is increased to $840,000.

The problem with section 2032A, however, like other tax-saving provisions, is that it requires certain conditions to be met. Further, even where those requirements can be complied with, the parties may consider them too onerous to be worth the tax benefit. Among the stipulations for 2032A to apply are the following:

- The decedent must be a resident or citizen of the United States.

- The property can only pass to certain members of the decedent's family.

- The decedent, or a member of the decedent's family, must have owned the property and materially participated in the operation of the farm or business for 5 of the 8 years before and after the decedent's death.

- The value of the real and personal property used in the farm or business must comprise at least 50% of the value of the decedent's gross estate.

- At least 25% of the value of the decedent's gross estate must be represented by the value of the farm or small-business real estate.

- If the decedent's family disposes of the property, or ceases to use it in the prescribed manner for the required period, the tax benefits are recaptured through the imposition of an additional tax.

While the theory of 2032A is not difficult to understand, it is extremely complicated to apply in practice. Consequently, if you have a client who is contemplating the use of 2032A to minimize estate taxes, have them seek the necessary expertise.

Family-Owned Business Interests

The 1997 act created Internal Revenue Code section 2033A. Pursuant to that provision, an executor could have elected to exclude up to a certain amount of qualifying family-owned business interests from the estate of a decedent who died after 1997. The excludable amount was $1.3 million, reduced by the estate-tax applicable exclusion amount for the year of the decedent's death.

This meant that as the applicable exclusion increased between 1998 and 2006, the excludable amount under section 2033A was to decrease. That interrelationship between the family-owned business exclusion and the estate-tax applicable exclusion would have caused an unexpected increase in the estate tax of some estates using the family-owned business exclusion. Consequently, the IRS Restructuring and Reform Act of 1998 corrected the problem. That was done by redesignating section 2033A as section 2057, and changing the "exclusion" to a "deduction" that allows executors to elect a maximum deduction of $675,000 within the following restrictions:

By redesignating section 2033A as section 2057, and changing he "exclusion" to a "deduction" that allows executors to elect a maximum deduction of $675,000 within certain restrictions.

- If the maximum deduction is elected, the decedent's exemption eqivalent is limited to $625,000.

- If less than the maximum deduction is elected, the dededent's exemption equivalent is increased by the excess of $625,000 over the amount of the deduction, but not over what would apply if the deduction were not taken.

The *General Explanation of Tax Legislation Enacted in 1998* or "Blue Book" that is prepared by the Congressional Joint Committee on Taxation explains the above rules as follows:

"For example, assume the decedent dies in 2005, when the (applicable exclusion) . . . is $800,000. If the estate includes qualified family-owned business interests valued at $675,000 or more, the estate-tax liability is calculated as if the estate were allowed a family-owned business deduction of $675,000 and the (applicable exclusion)…is limited to $625,000. If the estate includes qualified family-owned business interests of $500,000 or less, all of the family-owned business interests could be deducted from the estate, and the (applicable exclusion) . . . is $800,000. If the estate includes qualified family-owned business interests valued between $500,000 and $675,000, all of the qualified family-owned business interests could be deducted from the estate, and the (applicable exclusion) amount . . . is calculated as the excess of $1.3 million over the amount of qualified family-owned business interests. (For example, if the qualified family-owned business interests were valued at $600,000, the applicable exclusion . . . is $700,000.)

To qualify for the deduction, the family-owned business interest must comprise more than 50% of the decedent's gross estate and certain conditions, including the following, must be met:

- The principal place of business must be in the United States.

- The decedent must have been a citizen or resident of the United States.

- At least 50% of the business must have been owned by the decedent and members of the decedent's family. In addition, the requirement is met if the business is owned 70% by two families, or 90% by three families, as long as the decedent's family owned at least 30%.

- For five of the eight years proceeding the decedent's death, the decedent or a member of the decedent's family had to have owned and materially participated in the business.

- The decedent's heirs must actively particpate in the business for at least 5 years of any eight-year period within ten years after the decedent's death.

If, within ten years of the decedent's death, the business is disposed of, or the material participation requirements are not met, some or all of the tax

To qualify for the deduction, the family-owned business interest must comprise more than 50% of the decedent's gross estate and certain conditions must be met,

benefits must be repaid. The amount of the repayment varies from 20% to 100%, depending on how long after the decedent's death the event causing the repayment occurs.

Like Internal Revenue Code section 2032A, the concept of section 2057 is not difficult to understand, but is extremely complicated to apply in practice. Consequently, clients contemplating the use of 2057 will need to seek legal and accounting assistance with the necessary expertise. In any case, the 2001 Tax Act repeals the family-owned business interests deduction for decedents who die after 2003.

Installment Payment of Estate Tax on Farm or Closely Held Small-Business Property

If more than 35% of a decedent's adjusted gross estate consists of an interest in a farm or other closely held business, the executor may elect to defer payment of the estate tax attributable to the farm or business for 5 years (paying interest only), and thereafter pay the tax in equal installments over the next 10 years.

If more than 35% of a decedent's adjusted gross estate consists of an interest in a farm or other closely held business, the executor may elect to defer payment of the estate tax attributable to the farm or business for 5 years (paying interest only), and thereafter pay the tax in equal installments over the next 10 years. In addition, interest is payable at a special 4% rate on the first $1 million dollars of value for the estates of decedents dying before 1998. Pursuant to the 1997 Act, however, for decedents dying after 1997, interest is imposed at a 2% rate on the first $1,120,000 of value (for 2003) in excess of the applicable exclusion amount. The rate imposed on the balance of the value of the business is reduced to 45% of the rate applied to underpayments of tax. In addition, note that because of the 1997 act, the original $1,000,000 figure is adjusted for inflation after 1998 (rounded down to the next lowest multiple of $10,000), and interest payments for those dying after 1997 will not be deductible. Consequently, as of 2003 the original $1 million limit is increased to $1,120,000.

As previously stated, to qualify for this benefit under Internal Revenue Code section 6166, more than 35% of the decedent's estate must be comprised of the interest in the farm or other closely held business. In applying this rule it does not matter whether the interest is held as a proprietorship, partnership or corporation. It must, however, be operated as an active trade or business since a passive rental of property does not count.

In addition, the 2001 Tax Act made two changes with regard to the availability of using the installment payment provisions of IRC section 6166. First, the availability was expanded to include qualified lending and finance businesses and certain holding company stock. Secondly, the number of permitted partners of a partnership, or shareholders of an eligible corporation, was increased from 15 to 45. These changes are effective for the estates of those dying after December 31, 2001.

The problem with section 6166 is that, like sections 2032A and 2057, it puts limits on the family's use and disposition of the property in question. Further, section 6166 is not really a solution to an individual's estate-tax problems, as the tax is not decreased. Rather, it is at best a relief provision for the families of those individuals who fail to find a solution during their lifetime. Such solutions, as will be seen in subsequent chapters, frequently involve the use of life insurance.

The problem with section 6166 is that it puts limits on the family's use and disposition of the property in question. It is not really a solution to an individual's estate-tax problems, as the tax is not decreased. Rather, it is at best a relief provision for the families of those individuals who fail to find a solution during their lifetime.

CHAPTER 3

Estate-Tax Savings Through Gifting Programs

Estates Exceeding the Estate-Tax Applicable Exclusion Amount

Recognizing the scheduled increases in the estate-tax applicable exclusion amount that were brought about by the 2001 Tax Act, individuals with a net worth of $1,000,000 to $3,500,000 between 2002 and 2009 (and married couples with twice that amount) will face the possibility of federal estate-tax liabilities upon their deaths because their estates exceed the shelter of the exclusion. The only ways to avoid the tax are to dispose of the excess before death or to leave it to charity at death. Dispositions before death can be by way of personal consumption or gifts.

For those individuals and couples who have more than adequate means to take care of their own needs, a lifetime gifting program is a way of avoiding estate tax that may provide personal satisfaction and benefit to others. The problem, however, with seeking to avoid estate tax by making gifts is that the donor will be exposed to the gift tax, unless

The only ways to avoid the tax are to dispose of the excess before death or to leave it to charity at death. Dispositions before death can be by way of personal consumption or gifts.

they take advantage of the annual gift-tax exclusion and their gift-tax applicable exclusion.

Combining the Annual Gift-Tax Exclusion with the Gift-Tax Applicable Exclusion Amount

If an individual's or a married couple's gifts exceed the applicable annual gift-tax exclusions, the excess may be offset against their gift-tax applicable exclusion amount. For example, assume that a married couple gave each of their three children $52,000 for a total of $156,000. This would result in a gift to each child of $30,000 in excess of the amount that the parents can give gift-tax free by utilizing their combined annual gift-tax exclusions ($52,000 - $22,000). To avoid having to pay a gift tax on the $30,000 excess to each child, the parent's would offset the excess against their gift-tax applicable exclusion. Since each parent's share of the excess would be $15,000 per child (½ of $30,000) and there are three children, the reduction in each parents gift-tax applicable exclusion would be 3 x $15,000 or $45,000. Further, for every year that the gifts are repeated each parent's gift-tax applicable exclusion would drop by another $45,000. Consequently, if the gifts were continued for ten years, each parent's gift-tax applicable exclusion would be reduced by 10 x $45,000 or $450,000. This means that each of their remaining gift-tax applicable exclusions would be $1,000,000 – $450,000 or $550,000.

Coordinating the Gift-Tax Applicable Credit/Exclusion with the Estate-Tax Applicable Credit/Exclusion

It should be noted that between 2002 and 2009 the gift- and estate-tax applicable credits/exclusions are still "unified" to the extent of their overlap. This means that if an individual uses up their entire $1 million gift-tax applicable exclusion and dies before 2010, there will be a corresponding reduction in the amount of their estate-tax applicable exclusion that remains to offset estate tax at their death. For example, if an individual exhausts their $1 million gift-tax applicable exclusion and dies in 2009, when the estate-tax applicable exclusion is $3.5 million, they will have $2.5 million of estate-tax applicable exclusion remaining. ($3.5 million applicable estate-tax exclusion – $1 million gift-tax applicable exclusion.)

This raises the point that it might not make sense to execute gifts that would exceed an individual's $1 million gift-tax applicable exclusion. The reason is that doing so would cause a gift tax to be payable, whereas, waiting until the individual died could result in less, or no, estate tax being paid on such transfers because of the higher estate-tax applicable exclusion or repeal of the estate tax in 2010.

On the other hand, there may be situations where it would make sense to incur a gift tax. This would be the case where the individual has assets in excess of the estate-tax applicable exclusion and they are not expected to survive until repeal of the estate tax. In this regard, remember that we are facing two presidential and four congressional elections between the time of this writing and the scheduled repeal of the estate tax in 2010. With changing political fortunes, anything could happen including reinstatement of the estate tax for 2010. Further, keep in mind that if the president and congress do nothing, the present transfer tax structure will return on January 1, 2011. What all this seems to mean is that, for those who do not expect to see repeal for either political or health reasons, planning should focus on reducing the size of their estate to save estate taxes, at little or no gift-tax cost.

The Advantage of Making Taxable Gifts

In light of the above, and for those with estates in excess of the estate-tax applicable exclusion, it makes economic sense to continue gifting even after the annual exclusion and gift-tax applicable exclusion have been fully availed, and the donor will be required to pay a gift tax on further gifts. This is because gifting is

Gifting is a more cost efficient way of transferring property to heirs, than is leaving it to them at death. The reason being that when property is transferred by gift there is no gift tax on the related gift tax.

a more cost-efficient way of transferring property to heirs, than is leaving it to them at death. The reason being that when property is transferred by gift there is no gift tax on the related gift tax. Conversely, when property is transferred at death, there is an estate tax on the estate tax attributable to the property. (For more on this you should read "Life Insurance for the Liquid Estate," by Hillery James Gallagher, in the March 1992 edition of the *CLU Journal*.)

The cost advantage of making gifts, over leaving property at death, raises the question of why people should not simply consider giving all of their property away immediately before death. The answer is that the gift tax on all transfers made within three years of the decedent's death must be included in the decedent's estate. That has the effect of creating an estate tax on the gift taxes paid with respect to gifts made within three years of death and eliminates any related cost advantage of making the gifts.

Leveraging the Annual Gift-Tax Exclusion and the Gift-Tax Applicable Exclusion Amount

Reducing a person's gift-tax applicable exclusion to make gifts in excess of the annual gift-tax exclusion means that less of the person's estate-tax applicable exclusion will be available to offset the estate tax on the remaining estate at their death. This is not necessarily detrimental, however, because the estate and related estate tax are decreased by the amount of gifts that are made in connection with the use of the gift-tax applicable exclusion. In addition, with proper planning, every dollar of annual gift-tax exclusion and gift-tax applicable exclusion that is used can be leveraged so that more than a corresponding dollar of estate tax will be saved. This leveraging may be accomplished in two ways: (1) giving property that is expected to appreciate, and (2) giving property that is discounted in value.

Gifts of Appreciating Property and Estate Freezing

Gifting appreciating property leverages the effect of applying the individual's annual exclusion and gift-tax applicable exclusion because the growth in the value of the property from the date of the gift until the donor's death escapes inclusion in the donor's estate. In its simplest form, this just requires giving property that is expected to go up in value. A more sophisticated technique that applies to business interests is called estate freezing.

Estate Freezing

To gain an understanding of how estate freezing operates, assume that a father owns an incorporated business, with a single class of stock, that is worth $1,000,000. Assume further, that the business is expanding rapidly, and that the father would like to transfer the future growth to his two children, so that it will not be included in his estate. The father could accomplish his objective of freezing the value of his interest, and transferring future appreciation to the children at minimal transfer-tax cost by doing a corporate recapitalization. Under such an arrangement, the father would exchange his single class of stock in the corporation for preferred and common stock. He would then keep the preferred stock and give the common stock to the children as seen in the following Diagram #1.

DIAGRAM #1. Corporate Recapitalization

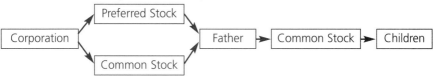

In creating the two classes of stock, the goal would be to design them so that most of the corporation's $1,000,000 of current value would be attributed to the preferred stock. This would have the effect of minimizing the value of the common stock given to the children and reduce the father's exposure to gift tax on that transfer. In addition, the two classes of stock would be structured so that any future appreciation in the value of the corporation after the recapitalization would be assigned to the common stock. That would operate to freeze the value of the father's preferred stock and allow future appreciation on the corporation to pass to the children through the common stock, without having such appreciation included in the father's estate.

Under section 2701 of the Internal Revenue Code, the preferred stock cannot be assigned a value that represents more than 90% of the value of the corporation.

Recognizing the transfer-tax benefits that can be derived by families from placing a high value on preferred stock in a recapitalization, Congress placed restrictions on how such stock can be valued. Under the current rules, preferred stock retained by a senior family member in a recapitalization is given a zero value for gift-tax purposes, unless it meets certain conditions. The consequence of being assigned a zero value for failing to meet the special requirements would be that all of the corporation's value would be attributed to the common stock. Using the facts in the above example, this would have the effect of exposing the entire $1,000,000 of corporate value to gift tax on the transfer of the common stock to the children. (Of course the father could use his annual gift-tax exclusions and gift-tax applicable exclusion amount as an offset against the gift tax.)

The special requirement that must be met, for the preferred stock to be assigned value, is that it carry a qualified payment right. Generally, this condition is satisfied where the preferred stock provides for a fixed-rate cumulative dividend that is payable on a periodic basis. The reason behind this requirement is that such a payment right is evidence that the preferred stock has value, since the senior family member will receive benefits from holding it. In any case, under section 2701 of the Internal Revenue Code, the preferred stock cannot be assigned a value that represents more than 90% of the value of the corporation.

Lack of Marketability and Minority-Interest Discounts

The idea behind leveraging with discounted gifts is to structure the transfer in a way that allows the value of the gift to be reduced before applying the annual gift-tax exclusion and the gift-tax applicable exclusion. That way more property can be transferred for the same amount of annual exclusion and gift-tax applicable exclusion. This depends upon structuring the gift as a business interest that qualifies for the lack of marketability and minority-interest discounts. As to how this concept operates, assume that a married couple owns a large farm worth $4,000,000 that they would like to pass on to their three children. Assume further, that they want to reduce their potential estate-tax liability on the farm, but they are currently unwilling to give up control of the property to the children.

Family Limited Partnership

If the parents were to form a family limited partnership, and transfer the farm to the partnership, in return for both limited and general partnership inter-

The idea behind leveraging with discounted gifts is to structure the transfer in a way that allows the value of the gift to be reduced before applying the annual gift-tax exclusion and the gift-tax applicable exclusion.

ests, they could make gifts of the limited interests to the children. This would permit the parents to reduce the size of their estates without losing control of the farm. The reason is that only the parents, as general partners, would have the powers to direct the distribution of income and principal from the partnership to themselves and the children. The structure of this arrangement may be seen in Diagram #2.

DIAGRAM #2. Family Limited Partnership

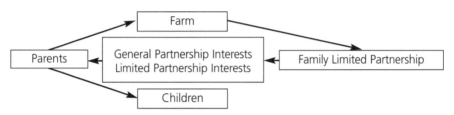

Only the parents, as general partners, would have the powers to direct the distribution of income and principal from the partnership to themselves and the children.

In addition, depending upon the facts of the case, the value of the interests transferred to the children may be reduced by as much as 35% for the lack of marketability and minority-interest discounts. These marketability and minority-interest discounts relate to the fact that a stranger to the family would not pay full price to acquire an interest in a business for which there is not a ready resale market, and in which they would have a noncontrolling interest.

From a leveraging perspective, what this means is that the discounts allow the parents to magnify the amount of property that they transfer to the children, gift-tax free, through utilization of their annual exclusions and gift-tax applicable exclusions. For example, if upon establishing the partnership in 2003, the parents were able to give the children limited partnership interests equal to the parents' combined annual exclusions and exemption equivalents, at a 35% discount, the children would receive $3,178,461 of undiscounted limited partnership interests. Without the discounts, the parents could only have transferred $2,066,000 gift-tax free ($2,000,000 of the parents' combined gift-tax applicable exclusions in 2003, plus $66,000 of their combined annual gift-tax exclusions for the year = $2,066,000). Consequently, the discounts allowed the parents to transfer an additional $1,112,467 of undiscounted value, using the same amount of annual exclusions and gift-tax applicable exclusions. Further, in subsequent years the parents could continue to make tax-free discounted gifts by utilizing their annual gift-tax exclusions. This would have a dramatic impact on the reduction of the parents' potential estate-tax liabilities, without generating any gift tax, or causing the parents to lose control of their property.

It should be noted, however, that because of certain abuses in this area, family limited partnerships are being scrutinized by the IRS. In that regard, the IRS has held that the value of the limited partnership interests, for estate-tax purposes, should be the pro rata value of the partnership, without any discount. While the ruling involved egregious facts, it is a reminder that the IRS is examining the transfer-tax consequences relating to family limited partnerships, particularly those cases it perceives as abusive. In that respect, when such a partnership is being considered, it is important that the partnership serve very important non-tax purposes which justify its creation aside from the transfer-tax savings.

Subchapter S Corporation

Another way for the parents to accomplish their discounting objectives would be for them to establish a Subchapter S corporation with voting and nonvoting stock. They could then give the nonvoting stock to their children, utilizing the lack of marketability and minority-interest discounts to leverage their annual gift-tax exclusions and gift-tax applicable exclusion amounts. An important factor in this regard is that the voting and nonvoting stock will not be considered as two separate

**Another way
for the parents
to accomplish
their discounting
objectives would
be for them to
establish a
Subchapter S
corporation
with voting and
nonvoting stock.**

classes of stock by the IRS. That is significant because a Subchapter S corporation cannot have more than one class of stock. Consequently, this approach to discounting can be employed without causing the corporation to lose its Subchapter S status.

Limited Liability Companies (LLCs)

A further development in making discounted gifts, is the use of limited liability companies (LLCs) in place of limited partnerships or corporations. This new form of business ownership has now been authorized in all states, and combines the limited liability protection of corporations with the pass-through income-tax advantage of a partnership.

The operating agreement of an LLC is similar to the shareholders' agreement and by-laws of a corporation and may permit the appointment of a "manager." The manager's powers are like those of a general partner in a family limited partnership, with the advantage that the manager does not have personal liability for the LLC. This means that the manager of an LLC may make gifts of interests in the LLC for purposes of reducing their estate, without giving up control of the LLC's underlying assets.

Split-Interest Gift Discounts

An additional approach to leveraging the annual exclusion and gift-tax applicable exclusion through discounting is based on the idea of splitting interests in property and then giving partial interests in the property to family members. The discounts come from taking advantage of differences between government tables that are used to value such partial gifts, and their actual value under circumstances where the government tables produce a lower figure than the property's actual value.

Conceptually, what the donor does is place income-producing property in a trust, and retain a right to income from the trust for a term of years. When the retention period ends, the remainder of the property in the trust passes to a family member(s). The structure of the arrangement may be seen in the following Diagram #3.

DIAGRAM #3. Split-Interest Discounts

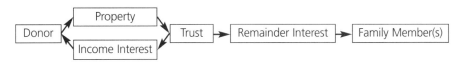

If the arrangement is properly structured, the value of the donor's income interest is measured in accordance with the government tables and deducted from the value of the property to determine the value of the remainder interest. If the property placed in the trust produces an income stream in excess of the rate assumed in the government tables, the remainder interest will be undervalued for gift-tax purposes. What this means is that the donor will be able to transfer the remainder interest at a discount for gift-tax purposes, and either use less of the donor's gift-tax applicable exclusion or pay less gift tax to remove the property from the donor's estate.

In order to keep the trust property, and any attendant appreciation, out of the donor's estate, the donor must survive the trust term. If the donor does not live through the required period, some, or all, of the trust's assets would be included in the donor's estate. The good news in such a situation is that any

The donor places income-producing property in a trust, and retains a right to income from the trust for a term of years. When the retention period ends, the remainder of the property in the trust passes to a family member(s).

reduction in the estate-tax applicable exclusion (through use of a corresponding amount of gift-tax applicable exclusion) that was used to set up the trust will be restored to the donor, and can be used to offset any estate tax. Further, if any gift tax was actually paid to set up the arrangement, it will be credited against any of the donor's estate-tax liability.

GRAT and GRUT Discounts

A grantor retained annuity trust (GRAT) provides the donor a fixed annuity payment each year, regardless of what happens to the value of the trust's assets.

In order to qualify for use of the government tables to value the remainder interest, the donor's retained income interest must be either a grantor retained annuity trust (GRAT) or a grantor retained unitrust (GRUT). A GRAT provides the donor a fixed annuity payment each year, regardless of what happens to the value of the trust's assets. On the other hand, a GRUT results in a variable annuity payment that goes up, or down, each year with the value of trust assets. A drawback of the GRUT is the need to revalue the assets annually, which may cause expense.

The situation where an individual should consider setting up a GRAT or GRUT is where they have an asset that they would like to temporarily retain the income from, but ultimately remove from their estate with minimal gift-tax consequences. In addition, the asset must be appreciating and capable of producing enough income to cover the promised payments to the individual. Further, the individual should be young enough to have a good probability of outliving a trust term that is long enough to provide a low present value for the remainder interest that constitutes the gift. Finally, the individual should be wealthy enough that they can part with the remainder interest without sacrificing their own financial security.

It should be noted that both GRATS and GRUTS probably constitute what are called "grantor trusts." This means that all the income from such trusts will be taxed to the individual who creates them, even if less than all of the trust's income is distributed to that individual. That is a positive result from a transfer tax saving perspective, however, since the income tax that is paid by the individual reduces their estate, and is itself a tax-free gift to the remainderman.

To cover possible estate taxes that could result if the individual dies before the end of the trust term, the purchase of life insurance should be considered, as a hedge, to pay any such tax. The insurance should not be owned by the insured, since it would be included in their estate. Rather it should be owned by a third party, like the remainderman, or another trust that is set up to pay estate taxes. This way, if the individual outlives the trust term, and no estate tax is due on the trust property, the life insurance can be used to pay any estate taxes on the individual's other assets.

On the other hand, a grantor retained unitrust (GRUT) results in a variable annuity payment that goes up, or down, each year with the value of trust assets. A drawback of the GRUT is the need to revalue the assets annually, which may cause expense.

Qualified Personal Residence Trust (QPRT)

Besides GRATS and GRUTS, an individual can take advantage of split-interest gifting at a discount by setting up a Qualified Personal Residence Trust (QPRT). Under such circumstances the individual transfers their home, apartment or vacation house to a trust, while retaining the right to live in it for a term of years, and leaving the remainder interest to someone else, like their children. The property owner may be the trustee of the trust. In addition, if they want to continue to live in the house after the end of the trust term, they may rent it from the remainderman without upsetting the transfer-tax savings as long as the rental is at the property's fair market value. How this arrangement works may be seen in the following Diagram #4.

DIAGRAM #4. Qualified Personal Residence Trust (QPRT)

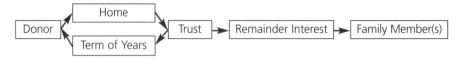

The amount of the gift is the value of the remainder interest, as determined by actuarial tables. Consequently, the gift-tax savings comes from using the value of the remainder interest, instead of the full fair-market value of the property to measure the amount of the gift. In this regard, the longer the term of retained use the lower the gift-tax value the remainder will have. The problem, however, is that a long period of retained use increases the probability that the individual will die during the trust term, and have the property included in their estate, which eliminates any tax saving.

A possible drawback to a QPRT is that the remainderman takes the grantor's income-tax basis for the property. This means that if the remainderman sells the property, he or she will have to recognize a capital gain, if the property has appreciated over the grantor's original basis. Conversely, if the remainderman simply inherited the property from the owner's estate, they would receive a step up in basis to the property's fair-market value at the owner's death. (This assumes that the grantor does not die in 2010.) Upon any subsequent sale, this step up in basis would produce a lower capital-gains tax for the remainderman than occurs under the QPRT. The bottom line is that due to the uncertainties of life in regard to the remainderman's need, or desire, to sell the property, the potential transfer tax saving from doing the QPRT should be compared to the possible additional capital-gains tax that could result from using the grantor's lower basis. In this regard, it should be noted that individuals may now exclude from taxation up to $250,000 of capital gain on the sale of a home, and married couples may exclude up to $500,000. This means that potential capital-gains taxes to the remainderman, on the resale of the home, may be reduced by the amount of the exclusion.

The creation of a GRAT, GRUT or QPRT is a gift of a future interest to the remainderman. Consequently, the gift of the remainder interest will not qualify for use of the grantor's annual gift-tax exclusion, and the grantor's gift-tax applicable exclusion will have to be applied to offset the gift tax generated by the transaction. In addition, special care must be exercised in regard to the generation-skipping tax, where the remaindermen are, or may be, skip persons (grandchildren or later generations). This is because the $1,120,000 GST exemption (for 2003) cannot be applied to the transferred property until the earlier of the end of the trust term, or the grantor's death. Consequently, because of the greater value for the remainderman's interest when the grantor's interest ends, or if the property in the trust appreciates between the trust's inception and the time when the GST exemption can be applied (called the estate-tax inclusion period) more of the exemption will have to be used to exclude the remainder from generation-skipping tax. To avoid this problem altogether, the grantor can simply limit the trust remainderman to his or her living children. That way, since there are no skip persons as remainder beneficiaries, there can be no generation-skipping tax exposure.

The bottom line is that due to the uncertainties of life in regard to the remainderman's need, or desire, to sell the property, the potential transfer tax saving from doing the QPRT should be compared to the possible additional capital-gains tax that could result from using the grantor's lower basis.

Charitable-Remainder Trusts

Another split ownership concept that can be used to reduce estate taxes is the charitable-remainder trust. This technique is particularly beneficial in those situations where an individual has a valuable asset with a low tax base, that is highly appreciated, but producing a low current rate of return. Typical examples would be undeveloped real estate, or publicly traded securities that a client would like to dispose of to purchase better-yielding assets, but is dissuaded from doing so because of potentially large capital-gains taxes.

Another split ownership concept that can be used to reduce estate taxes is the charitable-remainder trust. This technique is particularly beneficial in those situations where an individual has a valuable asset with a low tax base, that is highly appreciated, but producing a low current rate of return.

If the owner wanted to sell the property and invest the proceeds, they would first have to pay a capital gain tax of up to 20%, pursuant to the 1997 act (and maybe more due to state tax), which would substantially reduce the funds available for reinvestment. An alternative approach would be for the individual to establish a charitable-remainder trust, and transfer the property to the trust in return for an agreed amount of income each year for the rest of their life. The trust, as a charitable body, could then sell the property without having to pay a capital-gains tax, and reinvest the proceeds at a better rate of return. This would mean that the trust would have more to invest and could pay the individual a higher rate of return than they could have obtained by keeping, selling and reinvesting the property themselves. In addition, the individual would be entitled to an income-tax deduction for the value of the remainder interest given to the charity. (It should be noted that pursuant to the 1997 act, the value of the remainder interest must be at least 10% of the fair-market value of the assets initially contributed to the trust.) The value of that remainder interest would be calculated at the time the trust was established, on the basis of the life expectancy of the donor, and the rate of return to be paid him, or her, by the trust. Consequently, by combining the higher income flow and the tax deduction, the individual would have a substantially better cash flow than they did before establishing the trust. (The 1997 act also placed a limit on the amount that may be distributed to the non-charitable beneficiary each year. Depending upon which of two types of trusts are adopted, the non-charitable beneficiary may not receive more than either 50% of the initial fair-market value of trust assets, or not more than 50% of the annual value of trust assets.)

The only objection might come from the individual's family due to their concern about losing the value of the remainder interest to the charity. This problem could be cured by having the individual use a part of his, or her, increased income stream to purchase life insurance on themselves in an amount equal to the full value of the property transferred to the trust. The insurance should be owned from the start, and purchased through a separate irrevocable trust established by the individual for the benefit of the family. That way, the insurance would replace the property that went to the charity. In addition, by purchasing the insurance through an irrevocable trust, as will be explained later, the death proceeds may pass to the family income, estate, gift and generation-skipping tax free. The structure of the overall arrangement may be seen in the following Diagram #5.

By purchasing the insurance through an irrevocable trust, the death proceeds may pass to the family income, estate, gift and generation-skipping tax free.

DIAGRAM #5. Charitable-Remainder Trusts

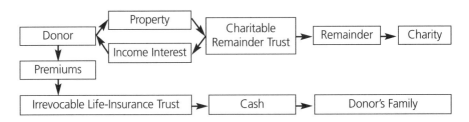

Charitable-Lead Trusts

A further form of charitable split-interest trust is the charitable-lead trust. These trusts are the opposite of charitable-remainder trusts in that the income stream is paid to one or more charities (either for someone's life or a term of years), and the remainder interest, is passed to one or more non-charitable beneficiaries, such as the donor's heirs. The structure of such an arrangement may be seen in Diagram #6 as follows:

DIAGRAM #6. Charitable-Lead Trusts

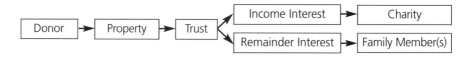

An advantage of establishing a lead trust is that the non-charitable remainder, that goes to the donor's family, is discounted for estate and gift-tax purposes, under IRS tables.

Unlike charitable-remainder trusts, lead trusts are not income-tax exempt. This means that any sale of donated assets will cause a capital gain, or loss, that might not be completely offset by any charitable contribution deduction that the trust would be entitled to for distributions to charity.

An advantage of establishing a lead trust is that the non-charitable remainder, that goes to the donor's family, is discounted for estate and gift-tax purposes, under IRS tables. Further, some or all of the appreciation on the trust property during the lead period passes to the donor's family without transfer tax. The principal disadvantage of these trusts is that the donor's family gives up the use of the property, and any income therefrom for the trust term. Consequently, these trusts are generally for families that do not have an immediate need for the use of the assets and related income.

Retirement Planning

Since qualified retirement plan benefits and IRA benefits that are payable after a decedent's death are includible in the decedent's gross estate, planning to minimize their tax impact should be considered. In that regard, the plan participant or IRA holder should consider accelerating the payment of the benefit, if possible, during their life. This would reduce their estate by the amount of income tax incurred on the benefits. They could then further reduce their estate by making gifts of any remaining cash. In any case, there is no substitute for crunching the numbers and any potential estate-tax savings should be compared to the growth on the funds from keeping them income-tax deferred, inside the pension plan or IRA.

Since qualified retirement plan benefits and IRA benefits that are payable after a decedent's death are includible in the decedent's gross estate, planning to minimize their tax impact should be considered.

Alternatively, the individual might name their spouse as the beneficiary for any qualified plan, and IRA benefits, upon their death. This would allow the surviving spouse to roll over the benefits which would defer the income and estate-tax liabilities. Further, the surviving spouse could name children, or other younger-generation individuals, as beneficiaries. While this would expose any remaining benefit to estate tax in the surviving spouse's estate, it would permit spreading out, even further, income tax on the benefits. Finally, the children, or other younger beneficiaries, would also be entitled to an income-tax deduction for related estate taxes paid by the deceased surviving spouse's estate. The family should be careful, however, that there are other assets available to pay the estate tax on the benefits. If no such assets are available, life insurance should be considered as a source of funds to pay any such tax liability.

Finally, since so much of any qualified plan or IRA benefits may be lost to income and estate taxes if the benefits are left to family members, the plan participant or IRA holder should consider naming a charity as beneficiary. This would avoid all income and estate tax on the benefits. Variations on this theme would be to name the surviving spouse, a QTIP trust or a charitable remainder trust. Under such arrangements, the surviving spouse could be provided lifetime benefits with any remainder going to the charity, income and estate-tax free.

CHAPTER 4

Providing Estate-Tax Liquidity With Life Insurance

Family and Trust-Owned Life Insurance

If, after an individual has utilized all the estate-tax saving techniques that they can, and want, to apply, there remains a future estate-tax liability, they should consider funding that obligation through the purchase of life insurance. That is because life insurance is cost-efficient, and has the unique advantage of providing the funds exactly when they are needed. This is at the time of the individual's death, when the tax becomes due. Here you should remember that if the person is married, all estate tax can be postponed until the deaths of both husband and wife through the utilization of the marital deduction. In such a case, the couple can purchase a second-to-die policy to match the timing of the death proceeds to the occurrence of the tax liability, at the second death.

If an individual purchases and retains ownership of a policy on their life that is acquired for any purpose, including to fund estate-tax liabilities, the death proceeds will be exposed to estate tax under Internal Revenue Code section 2042. Since the imposition of

Life insurance is cost-efficient, and has the unique advantage of providing the funds exactly when they are needed. This is at the time of the individual's death when the tax becomes due.

estate tax on the death proceeds would reduce the amount available to pay tax on the individual's other assets, it is a result that can, and should be, avoided. The price an insured must be willing to pay, however, to avoid estate tax on the proceeds, is giving up control of the policy. This can be done by transferring an existing policy to a third party, or by having the third party acquire the policy in the first place. The third party can either be a family member or an irrevocable trust. In this regard, ownership by a family member has the advantage of simplicity, but if several family members, such as children, are to own the policy together, a trust will probably be a more practical alternative. This is because if there are multiple owners, there is the potential for family squabbles that can frustrate the insured's objective of having obtained the coverage to pay taxes. Further, if there are minor children involved, there is little choice but to utilize a trust since an insurance company will not pay death proceeds to a minor.

Irrevocable Life-Insurance Trusts

Comparing the choices between having the proposed insured purchase the policy and having the trust acquire it, the better approach is to start with the trust. This is because the three-year rule of Internal Revenue Code section 2035 will apply to situations where coverage is purchased by the insured and transferred to the trust. That means if the insured dies within three years of the transfer to the trust, the death proceeds will be included in the insured's gross estate, and may be subject to estate tax. On the other hand, if the coverage is initially purchased by the trust, even if the insured dies within three years of the acquisition, the proceeds will not be included in his or her gross estate.

To implement such a plan the proposed insured should establish an irrevocable trust, and make gifts of cash to the trust with which the trustee can purchase the policy. To achieve certainty that the proceeds will not be included in the insured's estate, however, it is imperative that the trustee be the applicant, owner and beneficiary of the policy.

Applying the Annual Gift-Tax Exclusion

When making gifts to an irrevocable life-insurance trust, including to finance premium payments, it is desirable to have such gifts qualify for the annual gift-tax exclusion. This is because it allows the insured to give each trust beneficiary $11,000, or $22,000 per year, gift-tax free (depending on whether the insured is married). For example, a married insured who establishes a trust for his or her three children can give up to $22,000 to the trust for each child, for a total of $66,000 per year, gift-tax free.

Crummey Withdraw Rights

To qualify for the annual exclusion, however, the gifts must be considered gifts of present interests. That is deemed to happen, automatically, where the trust is designed so that the death proceeds must be paid by the trustee to the beneficiaries upon the insured's death. But that is not the usual design. If, however, the trustee is required to retain the proceeds after the insured's death, gifts to the trust will not qualify for the annual exclusion, unless the trust beneficiaries have been granted Crummey withdraw rights as to the gifts.

To achieve certainty that the proceeds will not be included in the insured's estate, however, it is imperative that the trustee be the applicant, owner and beneficiary of the policy.

The name Crummey comes from a court case, by that name, in which it was decided that where a beneficiary has a right to withdraw gifts to the trust, those contributions qualify as gifts of present interests. This approach works by providing in the trust instrument that when contributions are made to the trust, the trustee must notify the beneficiaries that they each have a right to withdraw their share of the gift. Under the terms of such trusts the power of withdrawal only exists for a limited period of time, such as 30 days. That window of opportunity is sufficient, however, to make the gifts to the trust gifts of present interests that qualify for the annual gift-tax exclusion.

The Cristofani Case

When the client's gifts to the trust exceed the amount of annual exclusions available under the trust, the client may offset the excess against their gift-tax applicable exclusion. Using the gift-tax applicable exclusion in this manner, however, means that there will be less of the estate-tax applicable exclusion left at the client's death to offset estate tax. Consequently, an alternative approach is to simply increase the number of annual exclusions by increasing the number of trust beneficiaries who have Crummey withdraw rights.

Example. Assume that a married couple establishes a trust for their three children to which they contribute $110,000 a year to cover the premium cost of a life insurance policy. If the three children have Crummey withdraw rights under the trust $66,000 (3 x $22,000) of the $110,000 annual gift will be excluded from gift tax because of the application of the couple's annual exclusions. To offset the $44,000

The name Crummey comes from a court case, by that name, in which it was decided that where a beneficiary has a right to withdraw gifts to the trust, those contributions qualify as gifts of present interests.

of excess premium, instead of reducing their gift-tax applicable exclusions, the couple could have drafted the trust to grant additional Crummey withdraw rights to a niece and a nephew. Under such an approach, the couple could completely offset their $110,000 annual gift with five sets of annual exclusions comprised of three for their children and two more for the niece and nephew.

The problem with this approach is that in order for the IRS to accept the legitimacy of the niece's and nephew's Crummey withdraw rights, those two individuals would have to be given additional rights to income or principal under the trust. This is because the IRS regards the granting of bare withdrawal rights, with no other interest in the trust, as a sham designed to simply increase the client's number of annual exclusions. The Service is fully aware that those who hold Crummey rights are generally not expected to exercise them, since to do so would defeat the purpose for which the trust was created. Fortunately, the Tax Court (a federal court in which tax cases may be fought without having to pay the tax first) disagreed with the IRS and upheld such bare Crummey withdraw rights in the case of *Cristofani v. Commissioner,* 97 T.C. 74 (1991). The Service announced its acceptance of the result of that case, but not the reasoning behind it. This means that any client who chooses the Cristofani approach to increase their number of annual gift-tax exclusions bears the risk that the IRS will challenge them in court. That is apparent from two actions on decision, and a technical-advice memorandum that the IRS has released on the subject, and which show that it will disallow annual exclusions for power holders who are mere contingent beneficiaries that do not hold vested interest in the income, or the corpus, of the trust.

The IRS regards the granting of bare withdrawal rights, with no other interest in the trust, as a sham designed to simply increase the client's number of annual exclusions. The Service is fully aware that those who hold Crummey rights are generally not expected to exercise them, since to do so would defeat the purpose for which the trust was created.

In addition, the IRS can be expected to oppose application of the annual exclusion where there is indication of an understanding that the beneficiaries will not exercise their withdrawal rights. In that regard, the Service lost on this issue in the case of *Estate of Kohlsaat v. Commissioner*, TC Memo 1997-212 (May 7, 1997) where the court refused to infer an agreement that the beneficiaries would not withdraw, from the mere fact that they did not exercise their rights.

Generation-Skipping Tax Considerations

Whenever an irrevocable life-insurance trust has grandchildren, or more remote descendants of the insured grantor as beneficiaries, there is a potential for generation-skipping tax liability. In such cases, the object of GST planning is to protect as much property as possible from the generation-skipping tax by using the GST exemption in the most advantageous way.

For trusts that are not designed to intentionally skip generations (such as trusts that are set up to provide funds to pay estate tax and are for the primary benefit of children, with grandchildren as contingent beneficiaries), generally no amount of the GST exemption should be allocated to gifts to the trust. Consistent with this objective, the automatic allocation of the GST exemption to indirect skips includes exceptions that are intended to prevent the automatic allocation of the exemption to such trusts. As previously noted, however, those exceptions may not be safely relied upon in all cases. Consequently, the terms of any life-insurance trust should be reviewed in light of the exceptions to the automatic allocation rule. If an exception is not clearly met, then the transferor should consider making an election to not

The object of GST planning is to protect as much property as possible from the generation-skipping tax by using the GST exemption in the most advantageous way.

have the automatic allocation apply. Subsequently, if there is a death out of order that would cause a generation-skipping tax, the transferor may make a retroactive allocation of the exemption, using the value of the property at the time of the original gift to the trust.

On the other hand, for trusts that are intended to benefit as many generations as possible without incurring a generation-skipping tax ("dynasty trusts"), the grantor's GST exemption should be applied to gifts as they are made to the trust. To that end, the terms of the trust should be examined to be sure that none of the exceptions to automatic allocation of the GST exemption apply. If the terms of the trust preclude automatic allocation of the GST exemption, the transferor should consider making an election to have the GST exemption apply.

After a trust becomes exempt from generation-skipping tax by the use of the GST exemption, no generation-skipping tax will be assessed on the trust as long as the property stays in the trust.

After a trust becomes exempt from generation-skipping tax by the use of the GST exemption, no generation-skipping tax will be assessed on the trust as long as the property stays in the trust. That duration, however, is governed in most states by the Rule Against Perpetuities which typically requires that trusts terminate no later than 21 years after the death of the last surviving beneficiary alive when the trust was established. Consequently, such a trust can last for nearly 100 years without any subsequent GST taxes. (Remember that under the 2001 Tax Act, the GST is only repealed for 2010, and returns on January 1, 2011.)

Paying the Estate Tax

If the trustee is required to use the death proceeds to pay the grantor insured's estate taxes, the proceeds so applied will be included in the grantor's estate and exposed to estate tax. To circumvent that problem, the trust should instead provide that the trustee has the authority to loan money to the grantor's estate, or to buy assets from it. This will give the estate liquidity without causing the proceeds to be included in the estate.

The trust should provide that the trustee has the authority to loan money to the grantor's estate, or to buy assets from it. This will give the estate liquidity without causing the proceeds to be included in the estate.

Example. Assume that an individual expected to have a $1 million estate-tax liability, and accordingly established a trust for his children to which he made gifts of cash with which to pay premiums. Upon the grantor insured's death, if the trust were required to use the $1 million of death proceeds to pay his estate tax, the proceeds would be included in his estate and exposed to estate tax. On the other hand, if the trust simply authorized the trustee to purchase assets from the grantor insured's estate, the trustee could buy $1 million of property from the grantor's executor. The executor would then have the $1 million in cash to pay the estate tax, and the trustee would have $1 million of property in the trust for the children's benefit. An illustration of how this works may be seen in Diagram #7.

DIAGRAM #7. Paying the Estate Tax.

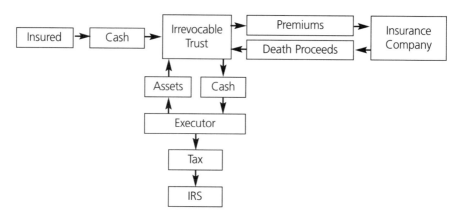

Considerations in Selecting a Trustee

The insured grantor should not be a trustee of the trust, since even powers held as a trustee could be deemed incidents of ownership that would cause the death proceeds to be included in the grantor's estate. The grantor may have the power to remove a trustee, and replace that trustee with another, as long as a new trustee is not a related or subordinate trustee, unless the related or subordinate trustee's powers are limited by an "ascertainable standard." This means that the grantor can replace a trustee with a related or subordinate trustee if the related or subordinate trustee can only make discretionary distributions to the trust beneficiaries for their maintenance, education, health and support (referred to as "MESH" powers). *See* PLR 200123034.

It should be noted that the IRS may even be expected to seek to include the proceeds of a trust in the estate of a beneficiary who has an unrestricted right to replace a trustee in a situation where the trust grants discretionary authority to the trustee to pay principal to the beneficiary. The IRS has, however, permitted a beneficiary to have such a power where it is triggered by certain limited circumstances beyond the beneficiary's control, such as the commission of a crime by the trustee, or the trustee's willful or negligent mismanagement of the trust.

Special Considerations for Trusts Holding Second-to-Die Policies

Where a second-to-die policy is placed in a trust, or acquired by the trust, care must be taken that neither insured could be considered to have incidents of ownership in the policy. Specifically, neither

The insured grantor should not be a trustee of the trust, since even powers held as a trustee could be deemed incidents of ownership that would cause the death proceeds to be included in the grantor's estate.

insured should be a trustee, beneficiary or have a Crummey withdraw right.

Buy and Sell Agreements

In the case of business interests, a way of providing liquidity to pay estate taxes on such property is to establish a life-insurance-funded buy and sell agreement. Another closely-related reason for having such an agreement is to fix the estate-tax value of the business interest. This is because without a predetermined value, the estate will have the burden of proving the accuracy of the figure that is claimed for estate-tax purposes. In addition, if the selling price, under the agreement, is less than the value determined to be correct for calculation of the estate tax, the estate would pay tax on value it did not receive. Finally, a penalty of 20% or more may apply where the value claimed on the return is one-half or less of the amount that is ultimately determined to be correct.

Requirements for Establishing Estate-Tax Value

The requirements for establishing the estate-tax value of a business interest, under a buy and sell agreement, have been developed through a combination of federal statutory and case law. Essentially, there are six conditions that must be met in order for the IRS to be bound by the value fixed in the agreement. They are as follows:

1. **The agreement must be a bona fide business arrangement.** This necessity is deemed to be met if the purpose of the agreement is to preserve family control and ownership of the business.

2. **The arrangement may not be a device to avoid taxes.** This refers to the concern that the agreement not be an attempt to make a tax-free transfer of the business interest to family members by way of an unreasonably low selling price. Consequently, the price must represent the fair market value of the seller's interest at the time of the agreement's execution.

3. **The agreement must be comparable to an arms-length arrangement between strangers.** Here again, the focus is on proving that the agreement is not a subterfuge for transferring property to family members under terms more favorable than would occur under comparable dealings between unrelated parties.

4. **The agreement must be a valid and enforceable contract.** This has to do with the question of whether the parties have observed all the formalities under state law for making the agreement a valid and enforceable contract. Further, they must respect the terms of the contract and treat it as something by which they intend to be legally bound.

5. **The agreement must be binding during the lives of the parties as well as at their deaths.** While alive, the parties may not dispose of their interests without either obtaining the consent of the other parties, or giving them the opportunity to match a legitimate offer. In addition, upon the death of a party, the agreement must give the survivors the option to purchase the decedent's interest, or require that the decedent's interest be sold to the survivors.

The requirements for establishing the estate-tax value of a business interest, under a buy and sell agreement, have been developed through a combination of federal statutory and case law. Essentially, there are six conditions that must be met in order for the IRS to be bound by the value fixed in the agreement.

6. The agreement must provide a fixed and determinable price for the parties interests.

This means that the agreement must provide some formula for determining the value of the parties interests upon sale during life, or at death.

Where the buy and sell agreement is between family members, all six of the requirements listed must be met to fix the estate-tax value of the participants' interests. In those situations, however, where the agreement is between individuals who have no family relationship, the first three requirements are automatically deemed to be satisfied.

Timing of Sale

When the focus of the buy and sell agreement is to provide estate-tax liquidity for a business owned by a married individual or jointly by a married couple, a question arises as to when the sale should take place. This is because of the ability to postpone all estate taxes on the value of the business until the deaths of both spouses through application of the marital deduction. If both spouses are involved in the operation of the business, and want to retain control of it until they are both dead, the sale can be postponed until the second death and funded through purchase of a second-to-die policy by the prospective purchaser or purchasers. This makes sense as long as each spouse is willing and capable of running the business after the other's death. Where, however, the survivor will lack the interest or capacity to continue the business, the sale should take place upon the first death, and might be funded with a first-to-die policy. Alternatively, if the business is completely owned by only one of the couple, a single policy on that person's life could be applied with an agreement requiring sale upon that person's death.

> When the focus of the buy and sell agreement is to provide estate-tax liquidity for a business owned by a married individual or jointly by a married couple, a question arises as to when the sale should take place. This is because of the ability to postpone all estate taxes on the value of the business until the deaths of both spouses through application of the marital deduction.

In those situations where the business owner wants to pass his or her interest on to the next generation, undiminished by estate tax, a second life insurance sale may be possible. That is because, in addition to the policy sold to the purchaser, there should also be considered a sale to the business owner of a policy to pay the estate tax on the value of their business interest. In such a situation, the life insurance acquired to cover the estate tax should be purchased through a third party to avoid the insurance being exposed to tax. As previously explained, this may be accomplished by having the life insurance bought by a family member(s) or an irrevocable trust.

Types of Agreements

Essentially, there are two basic types of buy and sell agreements. They are the entity purchase and cross-purchase arrangements. Under an entity agreement, the business contracts to purchase the owner's interest upon the owner's death, or has an option to acquire that interest, and the business owns the insurance to fund the purchase. Conversely, in a cross-purchase arrangement, the purchasers are individuals who typically have an interest in the business and they obtain life insurance on each other's lives to fund their acquisition of a deceased owner's interest.

Essentially, there are two basic types of buy and sell agreements. They are the entity purchase and cross-purchase arrangements.

A cross-purchase arrangement may be used for sole proprietorships, partnerships and corporations. On the other hand, an entity purchase arrangement applies to partnerships and corporations, but not to sole proprietorships. The reason is that sole proprietorships are not a separate legal entity from their owner, and therefore, do not have the capacity to contract. Consequently, in the case of a sole proprietorship, a cross-purchase agreement must be used, and the purchaser must be a legal entity such as another person, a partnership or a corporation.

Which Type of Agreement to Apply?

Each arrangement has advantages and disadvantages depending on the facts of the particular case. Some of the points to be considered are as follows:

- **Entity Purchase**

  This type of arrangement has the advantage of simplicity, since there is only one purchaser, which is the business. This means that there only has to be one life insurance policy on each person who has an interest in the business. A major disadvantage is that the surviving business owners' do not get a step up in basis for their increased shares when the purchase of a deceased owner's interest takes place. In addition, if the entity making the purchase, and owning the policies, is a corporation (other than a subchapter S corporation), the alternative corporate minimum tax is a consideration. This is because policy cash values and death proceeds figure in the calculation of the alternate tax. In that regard, the effect of the tax is minimized to the extent that it is not more than 15%, and may be offset against future regular corporate-tax liabilities. It should be noted that the 1997 act repealed the alternative corporate minimum tax for small-business corporations for taxable years after 1997.

  The following Diagram #8 illustrates the operation of an entity purchase arrangement between a business and its owners A and B, under circumstances where owner B dies after the arrangement is established.

This type of arrangement has the advantage of simplicity, since there is only one purchaser, which is the business. This means that there only has to be one life insurance policy on each person who has an interest in the business.

DIAGRAM #8. Entity Purchase Arrangement

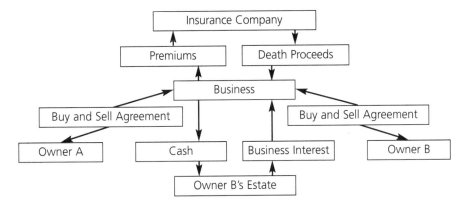

- **Cross Purchase**

  The major advantage of cross-purchase arrangements is that the surviving business owners' get a step up in basis for their interests. A significant drawback is that since there are multiple purchasers, there must be more than one policy on each business owner.

  A way to deal with the multiple policy problem is to have a trusteed cross-purchase arrangement, with the trustee owning a single policy on each person's life. For this to work, however, in a corporate situation, without causing problems with the transfer-for-value rule, each shareholder must be a partner in a separate partnership entity. That is because there is an exception to the transfer-for-value rule covering transfers of interests in a policy among partners. (A transfer-for-value is a transfer of any interest in a life insurance policy for a valuable consideration. The result is that the death proceeds in excess of the consideration, and subsequent premiums paid by the purchaser, are taxable income to the purchaser. Regarding a

The major advantage of cross-purchase arrangements is that the surviving business owners' get a step up in basis for their interests.

A significant drawback is that since there are multiple purchasers, there must be more than one policy on each business owner.

trusteed single-policy corporate cross-purchase arrangement, the transfer-for-value occurs on the death of a stockholder, as the deceased's interests in the policies on the survivors is shifted to the survivors.)

An example of how a cross-purchase arrangement works may be seen in Diagram #9. (Assume that the agreement is between owners A and B, and owner B dies after the agreement is implemented.)

Diagram #9. Cross-Purchase Arrangement.

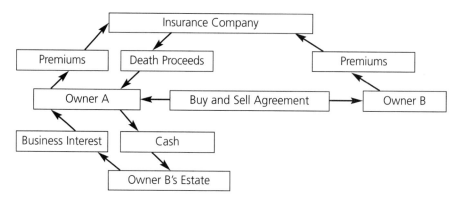

IRC Section 303 Stock Redemption Arrangement

IRC section 303 is an income-tax provision that allows a corporation to purchase a portion of a deceased stockholder's shares, with the redemption treated as a sale of the stock, rather than a taxable dividend. This is significant because to get such favorable income-tax treatment under a regular entity buy and sell agreement, all of the deceased stockholder's shares must be redeemed, rather than just a portion, as is permitted under section 303.

Consequently, section 303-type redemptions would have their greatest appeal where a family does not want to dispose of a decedent's entire stock interest, but needs funds from the redemption of some shares to meet estate liquidity requirements.

The special treatment of section 303 permits the estate to offset its basis for the shares that are sold (normally the fair market value of the stock at the shareholder's death) against the redemption proceeds with the result that there is little, if any, gain or loss on the transaction. Further, if there is any gain, it is taxed at favorable capital-gains rates rather than the regular income-tax rates that apply to dividend distributions.

To qualify for section 303 treatment, the deceased shareholder's stock must constitute more than 35% of his or her adjusted gross estate. In addition, the amount of redemption proceeds may not exceed the sum of the death taxes, funeral expenses and administration costs of the estate. The redemption must be on behalf of the beneficiaries, who are responsible for payment of the estate taxes and expenses. That requirement precludes a redemption by a beneficiary to whom the stock is specifically bequeathed, unless the beneficiary also is responsible for paying all, or part, of the taxes or expenses. Finally, any redemption must normally occur within three years and ninety days after the filing of the decedent's estate-tax return. There is an exception, however, where an election has been made under IRC section 6166. In such a case, redemptions may take place any time during the 15-year installment period. The operation of an IRC § 303 may be seen in Diagram #10 on the following page.

IRC Section 303 is an income-tax provision that allows a corporation to purchase a portion of a deceased stockholder's shares, with the redemption treated as a sale of the stock, rather than a taxable dividend.

DIAGRAM #10. Operation of an IRC Section 303.

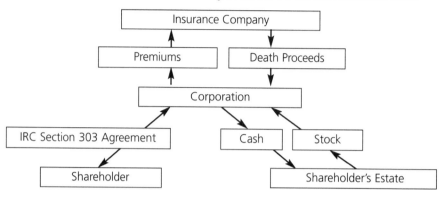

CHAPTER 5

Finding Premium Dollars

Often the most difficult part of implementing an estate plan is the search for premium dollars to fund the purchase of life insurance. In that regard, possible sources that should be considered are corporate-owned life insurance, split-dollar life insurance, IRC section 162 bonus plans and the liquidations of assets.

Corporate-Owned Life Insurance

Since the 1993 Tax Act, the top personal income-tax rate has exceeded the top corporate rate. The significance of this development, from an economic perspective, is that when given the choice between having nondeductible expenses paid by an individual, or their corporation, it is more cost-efficient to have the expenses paid by the party in the lower tax bracket. This means that where a proposed insured owns an incorporated business, and has a need for life insurance, their individual tax bracket should be compared to that of the corporation, and the insurance paid for by the corporation if it is in the lower bracket. An example of when such a situation would apply would be where a corporate owner needed life insurance to fund a buy and sell agreement. If the plan was set up as a stock redemption arrangement, the life insurance would be purchased and paid for by the corporation.

Split-Dollar Life Insurance

Another way of using corporate dollars to pay for life insurance is through the establishment of a split-dollar life insurance arrangement. For example, if a corporate owner needs life insurance to pay estate taxes, a split-dollar agreement could be set up between their corporation and a third party purchaser, such as a family member or an irrevocable trust. (Remember that the third party owner is used to keep the death proceeds out of the insured's estate.) An interesting aspect of such arrangements is that for gift-tax purposes, the gift is not the actual premium paid, but rather the imputed income attributed to the insured. This means that for those years that the imputed income is lower than the actual premium, the insured can cover a greater amount of life insurance with the same amount of annual gift-tax exclusion and gift-tax applicable exclusion amount. See IRS Notice 2002-8 and Split Dollar Proposed Regulations (REG 164754-01, 26 CFR Parts 1 and 31) for the impact that policy cash values may have for income and gift-tax purposes. Diagram #11 illustrates how a split-dollar arrangement may be set up between an insured's irrevocable trust and the corporation.

DIAGRAM #11. Split-dollar arrangement between an insured's irrevocable trust and the corporation.

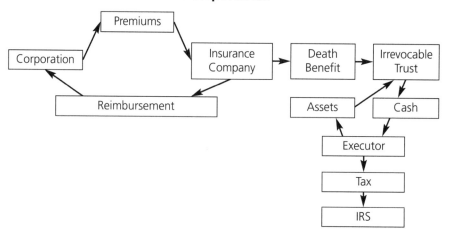

Split dollar can also be used to fund cross-purchase buy and sell agreements. In such situations, each party who purchases a policy on a stockholder would have a split-dollar agreement with the corporation to cover all, or part, of the premium cost. As a consequence of such an arrangement, each party holding a policy would have to recognize imputed income on the coverage. An illustration of how such an arrangement operates is shown in the following Diagram #12. (Assume that the corporation pays the entire split-dollar premium and that shareholders A and B have a cross-purchase buy & sell agreement, and that shareholder A dies after the agreement is in effect.)

DIAGRAM #12. Split dollar used to fund cross-purchase buy and sell agreements.

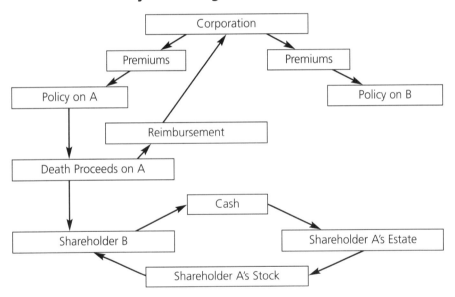

IRC Section 162 Bonus Arrangements

These are simply arrangements where a corporation pays the premiums on a life insurance policy owned by an employee who may also be a stockholder. The result is that the policy owner recognizes the premium as taxable income, while the corporation

IRC section 162 bonus arrangements differs from split-dollar arrangements on the corporate side, in that the corporation will not be repaid its premium advances, but will get a tax deduction for having made them.

deducts the same amount under IRC section 162 (which gives the arrangement its name). This approach to acquiring life insurance can be used any time life insurance is needed and the corporation can provide the funds. It differs from split-dollar arrangements on the corporate side, in that the corporation will not be repaid its premium advances, but will get a tax deduction for having made them. (Assuming the amount of the employee's total compensation is not unreasonable.) From the individual's perspective, it provides greater control of the policy, but at the cost of having to recognize a greater amount of taxable income for those years that the premium is higher than the imputed income under a split-dollar arrangement. The following Diagram #13 shows how this arrangement works.

DIAGRAM #13. IRC Section 162 Bonus Arrangements

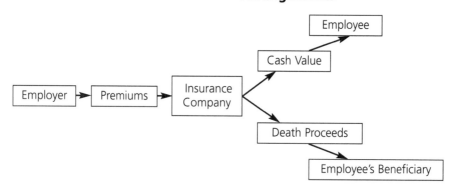

Liquidation of Assets

In some situations, individuals recognize the need for life insurance, and are willing to pay for it, but lack the cash flow to assume the responsibility for annual premiums. A prime example of that kind of client is a farmer or rancher facing a substantial estate-tax liability upon their death. In such situations, the client should consider selling a part of their property to purchase a single-premium policy that would protect the remainder of what they have from the estate tax. Otherwise, being in a forced sale situation, and without the benefit of prefunding, more of the property will have to be sold at their death to cover the tax. Further, not knowing when death will occur makes it difficult to plan an investment strategy that will precisely couple the availability of adequate funds to the time of death. Only life insurance can guarantee sufficient funds to match the timing of the estate-tax liability, regardless of when death occurs.

Only life insurance can guarantee sufficient funds to match the timing of the estate-tax liability, regardless of when death occurs.

CHAPTER 6

The Step-By-Step Estate Planning Process

Three Elements of Estate Planning

There are three parts to the subject of estate planning. They are:

1. Familiarity with the transfer tax laws and the estate-planning problems they present.

2. Knowledge of the available solutions to estate-planning problems.

3. Understanding the step-by-step process of analysis through which an individual's estate-planning problems, including the particular family situation, are identified and then matched to the appropriate estate-planning solutions.

So far, this book has dealt with the first two elements. You learned about the transfer-tax laws in Chapter 1, and covered estate-planning solutions in Chapters 2 through 5. There remains, however, the most important and interesting part which deals with mastering the process of analysis by which you can identify the individual's estate-planning problems, and match them to the appropriate solutions.

Element three deals with mastering the process of analysis by which you can identify the individual's estate-planning problems, and match them to the appropriate solutions.

You may wonder why it is so important to learn this process. The answer is that the process is what ties everything together in serving your clients. Consequently, the purpose of this chapter is to focus on that process by walking you through its specific steps. Then, in the next chapter, you will cover a case study through which you will see how those steps are actually applied in developing a comprehensive estate-planning proposal for a client.

Process of Analysis

By process of analysis, I mean a series of clearly identifiable steps that you go through in developing an estate planning proposal for any client. Those steps are as follows:

STEP 1. Gathering the Relevant Facts about the Client

There are certain types of facts that are generally relevant no matter who your client is.

There are certain types of facts that are generally relevant no matter who your client is. Those facts are the ones that are pertinent to the universal goals of conserving and transferring the client's estate to subsequent generations, at the lowest tax cost possible, while taking care of the client's own lifetime needs. Examples of such facts are:

- Who are the natural objects of the client's bounty, and what are the various family relationships?
- What does the client own?
- How is the client's property owned (i.e. sole ownership, joint ownership, held in trust, etc.)?
- What is the client's property worth, and what is its tax base?
- What is the client's income?

STEP 2. Identifying and Prioritizing the Client's Objectives

Frequently your clients will not have any estate-planning objectives because they have not thought about the subject, or if they have, they are not aware of the problems they face in reaching their goals. Your role in such a situation is to get them to think about their objectives, and, paying attention to the particular family dynamics, help them set their priorities. You do this by getting them to discuss the universal goals of conserving and transferring their estate at the lowest tax cost possible, while taking care of their own lifetime needs. When you do this, you will find that the usual order of priorities is as follows:

Your role is to get your clients to think about their objectives, and, paying attention to the particular family dynamics, help them set their priorities.

• **Meet the client's living needs for the rest of their life.** This is not a selfish goal for the client. Before a client can reasonably be expected to take care of someone else, they must be able to meet their own needs.

• **Address the needs of the client's family.** After taking care of the client's own lifetime needs, the next issue is determining how to meet the financial requirements and individual needs of members of the client's family. This most particularly includes a plan for dealing with the family's needs after the client dies.

• **Provide a plan for the distribution of the client's assets after the client's death.** After the client dies, the assets that were necessary to take care of the client's own lifetime needs will be free for distribution to other people or institutions the client wants to benefit after his or her death.

- **Save taxes.** The goal is to reduce income and transfer taxes so that there is more of the client's wealth left to meet the client's objectives.

- **Provide liquidity.** After the client has taken advantage of the available estate-tax saving techniques, life insurance should be considered as a timely and cost-efficient way of covering any remaining tax, or other liabilities, or providing for financial needs of family members.

STEP 3. Recognizing Determinative Facts

The determinative facts are important because they weigh heavily in selecting the estate-planning techniques that can and cannot be used in reaching the clients goals.

Here you must find the particular personal, financial and tax problems facing the client and the client's family in light of the client's goals of conserving and transferring the client's estate to future generations, at the lowest tax cost possible, while taking care of the client's lifetime needs. These determinative facts are important because they weigh heavily in selecting the estate-planning techniques that can and cannot be used in reaching the clients goals. Examples of what should be considered are:

- Who does the client want to receive property upon the client's death? Further, what kind of property and how much?
- What gifts has the client made during his or her lifetime?
- What gifts can the client afford to make?
- What will the estate tax be at the client's death?
- What is the liquidity of the client's estate?
- Has the client used any of his or her applicable credit amounts?
- Are there any business or property interests that require a plan of transition to new owners, and how will the transfers be funded?

STEP 4. Matching the Appropriate Estate-Planning Solutions to the Client's Problems

In this final step the inventory of estate-planning techniques is reviewed to find those that match the client's needs, and which are solutions the client is willing and able to apply. A summary of those techniques that have been described in earlier chapters, and should be considered, are as follows:

In this final step the inventory of estate-planning techniques is reviewed to find those that match the client's needs, and which are solutions the client is willing and able to apply.

Non-Gifting Techniques to Reduce Estate Taxes

- Will with by-pass trust and unlimited marital deduction
- Bracket shifting (paying some estate tax upon the first death)
- IRC Section 2032A Lower valuation of real estate in a farm or closely held business
- IRC Section 2057 Family-Owned Business deduction (not available after 2003)
- IRC Section 6166 Installment payment of estate tax

Gifting Techniques to Reduce Estate Taxes

- Gifts utilizing the annual gift-tax exclusion and the gift-tax applicable exclusion amount
- Leveraging the annual gift-tax exclusion and gift-tax applicable exclusion amount
- Gifts of appreciating property
    Estate freezing
- Lack of marketability and minority interest discounts
    Family limited partnerships
    Subchapter S corporations
    Limited liability companies

- Split-interest gifts
    GRAT, GRUT and QPRT
    Charitable-remainder trusts
    Charitable-lead trusts
- Retirement planning

Paying Estate Taxes with Life Insurance
- Family and trust-owned life insurance
- Life insurance funded buy and sell agreements
    Entity purchase
    Cross purchase
    IRC section 303

Sources of Premium Dollars
- Corporate-owned life insurance
- Split-dollar life insurance
- IRC section 162 Bonus arrangement
- Liquidation of assets

CHAPTER 7

Case Study

Factual Situation

Bill and Sue Smith are age 65 and married with four adult children: James, age 43; John, age 41; Jane, age 38; and Janet, age 33. All the children are married, and each have two children of their own.

Bill and Sue each own 50% of the stock of Smith Printing, a company (C corporation) they built from scratch over the last 40 years. The total fair market value of their Smith Printing stock is $5,000,000. Bill is CEO and Sue is Secretary/Treasurer. Their sons James and John are Vice Presidents of Marketing and Production, respectively. The sons have both worked in the business since finishing college, and want to take over the firm after their parents' deaths. Jane is the director of the Art Department and while she enjoys her job, she has no particular interest in having a greater role in the business. Finally, Janet, who is a teacher, has no desire to be involved in the business, except that her husband Tom has a middle-management position in the Production Department that provides an important part of their income.

Bill and Sue intend to retain control and stay involved in the business for the rest of their lives, but would like their two sons to take over after their deaths. Further, they are amenable to doing what is necessary, financially, to make their sons' acquisition of Smith Printing possible. At the same time, they want to be fair to their two daughters, so that their daughters end up with as equal a share of their estate as their sons.

Bill and Sue own a 500-acre farm that they inherited from Sue's parents. When they acquired the property, at the parents' deaths, it was worth $1,000 an acre and now has a fair-market value of $2,000 per acre. While the family intends to keep the property, they have no interest in operating it as a farm, and prefer to simply use it as a retreat.

Bill and Sue also own an unimproved parcel of land they bought 15 years ago, for speculative purposes, that cost them $50,000 and is now worth $500,000. They are no longer interested in keeping the property, and would like to do something with it to benefit their college alma mater. They are hesitant, however, about making such a large gift because of the potential income they would be giving up and their concern about so significantly reducing the childrens' inheritance.

In terms of life insurance, an old friend, who was an agent, recommended that Bill and Sue each acquire a $250,000 policy on their lives to help pay for estate taxes. They did this 15 years ago when the business was worth considerably less, and have not thought much about estate planning and transfer taxes since. They are concerned, however, about what would happen if they were both to die before 2010, and their combined estates were exposed to estate taxes. Consequently, they are interested in what can be done to reduce their estate-tax exposure, while providing liquidity to pay any estate taxes that might be incurred. Bill and Sue each own the policy on their life and the policies each have a cash value of $80,000.

Bill and Sue are very fond of their eight grandchildren and would like to establish a fund of some type for their benefit. In addition, they are particularly concerned about the financial security of their daughter Janet, since her income as a teacher is modest. Also, if something happened to Tom she would need assistance.

Step 1: Gathering the Relevant Facts

Individuals who regularly do estate planning typically have a fact gathering sheet that they use when they interview clients. Such a sheet will cover the types of questions described earlier, and since it is already prepared, the estate planner is less likely to overlook getting any important facts. At a minimum, such a sheet will list the members of the family and the client's principal assets and liabilities. Applying this approach to our case study the fact sheet would contain the following:

Family Data

Name	Relationship	Age
Bill	Father	65
Sue	Mother	65
James	Son	43
John	Son	41
Jane	Daughter	38
Janet	Daughter	33

Financial Data

Property	Bill	Sue	Joint
Smith Printing Stock	$2,500,000	$2,500,000	
Farm			$1,000,000
Unimproved land			$500,000
Life insurance cash value	$80,000	$80,000	
Home			$500,000

STEP 2. Identifying and Prioritizing the Client's Objectives

Considering their assets and what they have said they would like to do for themselves and their family, Bill and Sue have the following objectives in order of priority:

- Keep control of the business until both are deceased and then transfer it to their two sons with some financial assistance in the process.

- Derive a source of income from the unimproved real estate while benefiting their alma mater but not reducing their childrens' inheritance.

- Retain the farm for the family's benefit as a retreat.

- Provide Janet some current economic security in case something unfortunate happens to her husband.

- Do something for the grandchildren.

- Minimize transfer taxes and provide estate-tax liquidity.

STEP 3. Recognizing Determinative Facts

Bill and Sue have not utilized any of their gift-tax applicable exclusions through lifetime gifts. This is very important in that it gives them the option of using their full estate-tax applicable exclusions to set up by-pass trusts in their wills. Alternatively, they can use their gift-tax aplicable exclusions to offset gifts in excess of their annual gift-tax exclusions. That would be significant if they choose to make gifts as a way of minimizing their potential estate-tax liabilities. As for annual exclusions, just counting family members, they have four children and eight grandchildren which makes a total of 12. This means by splitting gifts they can give 12 x $22,000 or $264,000 a year to family members free of gift tax, and without touching their gift-tax applicable exclusions. Some of these transfers will be used in conjunction with life insurance premium payments as described hereafter.

Bill and Sue have not utilized any of their gift-tax applicable exclusions through lifetime gifts. This is very important in that it gives them the option of using their full estate-tax applicable exclusions to set up by-pass trusts in their wills. Alternatively, they can use their gift-tax aplicable exclusions to offset gifts in excess of their annual gift-tax exclusions.

In addition, Bill and Sue have not applied any of their $1,120,000 generation-skipping tax exemptions. This will be important if they choose to make gifts to their grandchildren, since application of their $1,120,000 exemptions will make such gifts free of generation-skipping tax.

Regarding potential estate-tax liability, Bill and Sue have combined estates of $7,500,000 (including life insurance death proceeds). Consequently, if they did nothing but utilize the by-pass trust/marital deduction approach under their wills, and both died in 2003 when the estate-tax applicable exclusion is $1,000,000, they would have $2,640,000 of estate tax upon the survivor's death.

Considering the farm property that they want to keep in the family, it has a basis of $1,000 per acre, and a fair-market value of $2,000 per acre. That means the farm would generate a capital gain of $1,000 per acre or $500,000 if the property were sold using the basis at which Bill and Sue inherited it. Conversely, if it were included in their estates it would receive a stepped up basis to fair market value at their deaths (unless they died in 2010). In that case, any capital gain on a subsequent sale by the children would be reduced or eliminated.

As to the undeveloped property, if Bill and Sue were to sell it they would have a capital gain of $450,000 ($500,000 fair-market value - $50,000 basis). This means that assuming a 20% rate, a capital-gains tax of $90,000 would have to be paid from the proceeds, leaving a net amount for investment of $410,000 ($500,000 - $90,000).

STEP 4. Matching the Appropriate Estate-Planning Solutions to the Client's Problems

Considering the implications of the determinative facts described under Step 3, appropriate solutions to Bill's and Sue's estate planning problems that may be suggested are as follows:

Maintaining control of the business and passing it on to the sons

- **Write their wills to leave each other their stock.**

- **The transfer of stock to the surviving spouse qualifies for the marital deduction.**

- **Enter into a cross-purchase buy and sell agreement with James and John.**

- **Enter into an employer-pay-all split-dollar agreement with Smith Printing on the second-to-die policy.**

Since Bill and Sue want to keep control of the business until they are both deceased, they should write their wills to leave each other their stock. This arrangement puts all the stock in the hands of the survivor, who can control the business until their death. That is consistent with the first priority of most older clients, which is to take care of themselves for the remainder of their lives, before thinking about passing on wealth to their families. Further, since the transfer of stock to the surviving spouse qualifies for the marital deduction, it will not be diminished by estate tax.

Having assured their lifetime financial security through control of Smith Printing, Bill and Sue could move on to their next priority of leaving the business to their two sons. To accomplish this they should enter into a cross-purchase buy and sell agreement with James and John. To fund the purchase of the stock the sons should acquire a $5,000,000 second-to-die policy on their parents. Further, since the parents want to provide some financial assistance to the sons to facilitate their taking over the business, the sons should enter into an employer-pay-all split-dollar agreement with Smith Printing on the second-to-die policy.

Derive a source of income from the unimproved real estate, while benefiting their alma mater but not reducing their childrens' inheritance

This is a perfect situation for a charitable-remainder trust. Bill and Sue should establish such a trust and transfer the property to it. Then the trust could sell the property without incurring the $90,000 capital-gain tax that Bill and Sue would have to pay if they sold the property themselves. This would enable the trust to pay them a higher rate of return than they could obtain themselves, with fewer dollars to invest. Bill and Sue would also be entitled to an income-tax deduction for the value of the remainder interest.

The combination of income payments from the trust and their offsetting charitable deductions would leave the parents in a better cash-flow position than before the trust was established. There would remain, however, the concern about reducing the childrens' inheritance by the loss of the remainder interest to the college. That could be solved by having Bill and Sue establish an irrevocable trust, funded with a $500,000 second-to-die policy. This way, upon their parents' deaths, the children would inherit $500,000 cash (estate and income-tax free), instead of the unimproved real estate. To avoid gift tax on transfers of cash to the irrevocable life-insurance trust, Bill and Sue could utilize their annual gift-tax exclusions.

- **Establish a charitable-remainder trust.**
- **Establish an irrevocable trust funded with a $500,000 second-to-die policy.**
- **Consider having the trust enter into a employer pay-all split-dollar agreement with Smith Printing.**

As a way of reducing the value of their gifts to the irrevocable life insurance trust, for purposes of applying their annual gift-tax exclusions, Bill and Sue should consider having the trust enter into a employer pay-all split-dollar agreement with Smith Printing. In that case the amount of the gifts to the trust would be measured by the imputed income, rather than the actual cash premiums.

Retain the farm for the family as a retreat
Considering the IRS's current critical view of the subject, a solution to this objective would be for Bill and Sue to establish a family limited partnership. They should each keep a general partnership interest to

retain managerial control of the property for their lifetimes. Further, by limiting the value of each of the general partnership interests to 1% of the property's $1,000,000 value, $980,000 could be placed in limited partnership interests for transfer to the children. Then, assuming a 35% discount rate and splitting the gift between them, Sue and Bill could transfer the entire $980,000 of limited partnership interests to the children for just $637,000 of their gift-tax aplicable exclusions ($318,500 each). That would get the farm out of their estates at a substantial discount in value, which would represent a minimal use of their gift-tax aplicable exclusions.

A possible drawback to this approach would be that since the property would not be included in the parent's estates, the children would not get a full step up in basis to its fair-market value at the parents' deaths (assuming they died before 2010). That would be significant if the children were going to sell the property, since it would mean a substantial capital gain would be incurred. Since, however, the family intends to keep the property as a retreat, capital gain would not be a concern.

Provide Janet some current economic security, in case something unfortunate happens to her husband

A way of providing security to Janet would be for Smith Printing to establish a IRC section 162 bonus arrangement for her husband. In such a case, the company would pay the premiums on a policy purchased by the husband on his own life, naming Janet the beneficiary. The company would get a tax deduction for the premium payments and Janet's husband would recognize the amount of the premi-

* **Establish a family limited partnership.**
* **Keep a general partnership interest to retain managerial control of the property for their lifetimes.**

* **Establish a IRC section 162 bonus arrangement.**

ums as taxable income. This means that Bill and Sue would not have to worry about making a taxable gift to Janet to provide her the desired security. Further, if they want to relieve Janet and her husband of the burden of paying the income tax on the premium, they could bonus the husband an additional amount to pay the tax.

Do something for the grandchildren

Bill and Sue each own a $250,000 policy on their own life. If they retain ownership of these policies, the death proceeds will be included in their estates and a substantial portion of the proceeds will be lost to estate taxes. Since they want to benefit their grandchildren, and should get the policy proceeds out of their estates, they should establish an irrevocable trust for the grandchildren and transfer the policies to it. Estate tax will be eliminated, assuming they live for more than 3 years after the transfer. Since there are eight grandchildren, and they can give each one $22,000, their annual gift-tax exclusions will more than cover the policies' cash values of $160,000. That means there will be no gift tax or reductions in Bill's and Sue's gift-tax applicable exclusions on the transfer.

• Establish an irrevocable trust for the grandchildren and transfer the policies to it.

Since the transfer of the policies to the trust will be a direct skip for purposes of the generation-skipping tax, $80,000 of each of their $1,120,000 GST exemptions will be automatically applied to the transfer. In addition, as they make gifts to the trust each year to cover premium payments, that amount will be automatically applied against their $1,120,000 GST exemptions (½ to each) to cover the premiums. This way the entire $500,000 of death proceeds will be exempt from generation-skipping tax.

- **Establish by-pass trusts in each of their wills in the amount of their remaining estate-tax applicable exclusions, with the balance of their estates passing under the marital deduction.**

Minimize transfer taxes and provide estate-tax liquidity

In setting up the family limited partnership for the farm, Bill and Sue would each use $318,500 of their gift-tax applicable exclusions. Assuming they both die between 2003 and 2009, when the estate-tax applicable exclusion will be between $1,000,000 and $3,500,000, this would leave between $681,500 and $3,181,500 that could be availed of to establish by-pass trusts in each of their wills. Consequently, their wills should be drafted to provide for the creation of by-pass trusts in the amount of their remaining estate-tax applicable exclusions, with the balance of their estates passing under the marital deduction. This would eliminate any estate tax on the death of the first to die, and shelter the amount of remaining estate-tax applicable exclusion in that decedent's by-pass trust from estate tax on the survivor's death.

Alternatively, Bill and Sue could consider bracket shifting by not fully utilizing the marital deduction under their wills. The problem with that approach, however, is that it would require the payment of a substantial amount of estate tax on the first decedent's death and neither estate is liquid. Consequently, it is very unlikely that Bill and Sue could be convinced that the potential estate-tax savings would be worth the sacrifice of paying so much tax upon the first death.

Finally, after reducing Bill's and Sue's estates through the above techniques, their combined estates would be worth $5,520,000, calculated as follows:

Smith Printing	$ 5,000,000
Farm general partnership interests	$ 20,000
Home	$ 500,000
Total	**$ 5,520,000**

Assuming they both died in 2003, taking advantage of their combined remaining estate-tax applicable exclusions of $1,363,000, and choosing not to utilize IRC section 2057 (Family-Owned Business deduction), they would have a potential estate-tax liability, upon the death of the survivor, of $1,887,840. The $5,000,000 of second-to-die proceeds that would be received by the executor of the survivor through the buy and sell agreement with the sons would be more than sufficient to pay the tax leaving a balance of $3,112,160. This cash could be left to Janet and Jane to partially compensate them for the effect of the business (valued at $5,000,000) going to the two brothers. The rest of the parent's estate could then be divided equally among the children or left to the daughters, as the parents decide.

CHAPTER 8

Elder Law

Aging U.S. Population

As was stated in Chapter 1, estate planning is not just concerned with minimizing and paying transfer taxes. Rather, it also focuses on taking care of a client's needs due to aging, in later life.

In response to this, a body of law has developed that concentrates on the needs of older Americans. Called Elder Law, it centers, in part, on the interplay between our senior citizens' personal finances and public programs such as Social Security, Medicare and Medicaid. In addition, it covers concerns over how to deal with their property, and health care decisions when their ability to care for themselves is significantly impaired through advanced age or illness.

Since this book is not devoted to the subject of personal finance, public programs will not be discussed. What will be dealt with, however, are those issues involving how to take care of a person's health and property, when they are unable to make decisions for themselves. That is because such problems are excellent door openers to the broader subject of estate

This chapter will focus on the types of documents which are used to effectuate a persons wishes in the areas of property and personal health care management when they are legally incompetent. Those documents are:

- **Durable Powers of Attorney**
- **Advance Directives**
- **Revocable Living Trusts**

planning, which can lead to the provision of services and products described in earlier chapters. This chapter will focus on the types of documents which are used to effectuate a person's wishes in the areas of property and personal health-care management, when they are legally incompetent. Those documents are Durable Powers of Attorney, Advance Directives and Revocable Living Trusts.

Durable Powers of Attorney

A Durable Power of Attorney — prepared before a person becomes incompetent — authorizes a spouse, or other family member, to handle their property matters.

Once a person becomes legally incompetent, the only way to arrange for the management of their property is to go through a court proceeding to have a conservator, or guardian, appointed. Unfortunately, this tends to be a relatively expensive and time-consuming process that is also an unpleasant experience for the incompetent's family. Generally, a much simpler and effective alternative is to have the elderly individual prepare a Durable Power of Attorney before they become incompetent, authorizing a spouse or other family member to handle their property matters.

A Power of Attorney is a document that authorizes one person (the attorney in fact) to deal with the property of another person (the principal). In the absence of a provision to the contrary, such powers automatically cease on the principal's becoming incompetent. In that regard, all 50 states have enacted statutes permitting the creation of Durable Powers of Attorney that do not cease upon the principal's incompetence, providing that language to such effect is included in the document. Consequently, a Durable Power can be used to protect a principal's property during a period of incompetence, without the necessity of seeking a court-appointed conservator.

The various state forms for creating Durable Powers of Attorney do not address all the possible situations that might arise with regard to a particular principal. This means that a lawyer should be consulted to draft the document in light of the principal's particular circumstances, and objectives, in creating the Power. Further, when possible, the individuals and institutions that might be expected to honor the Power should be consulted as to its terms in case they have special requirements.

A useful variation of Durable Powers of Attorney, that is permitted in some states, is called a Springing Power of Attorney. This type of document provides that it takes no effect until the principal becomes incompetent. It is appropriate in those situations when the principal does not want to authorize anyone to deal with their property until they are unable to do so for themselves.

An alternative is for the individual, before becoming incompetent, to create a Revocable Living Trust, and fund it with their assets. This is discussed later on in this chapter.

A useful variation of Durable Powers of Attorney, that is permitted in some states, is called a Springing Power of Attorney. This type of document provides that it takes no effect until the principal becomes incompetent.

Advance Directives

The development of advances in medical science have made it possible to prolong human life to the point that conflicts arise with regard to personal values. Nonetheless, our law gives patients the right to determine the level of care they want, under the doctrine of informed consent. That theory is based on the idea that people should decide for themselves critical medical issues after informed discussion with their physicians. This concept of individual choice has also been extended to those who are legally incompetent at the time of treatment. The problem presented in such cases is one of determining what course the patient would choose, under circumstances where they cannot effectively communicate.

Living Wills

To answer this problem, some state legislatures have responded with laws permitting individuals to make advance directives which are written documents evidencing the person's predetermination of the medical treatments they will, and will not, accept under circumstances when they are legally incompetent. One type of instrument is commonly called a Living Will and it typically focuses on three major issues, such as the patient's willingness to accept:

1. Artificial nutrition and hydration
2. Pain-killing drugs
3. Extraordinary procedures

A criticism of Living Wills is that they only apply to the terminally ill, and are limited to decisions to withhold or withdraw life-sustaining treatment.

Health Care Proxy

This form of document, sometimes described by other names, is used where permitted by state law to deal with the shortcomings of Living Wills. This is accomplished by allowing an individual to appoint another person or proxy to make medical decisions for them that are not restricted to life-sustaining treatment. Further, under some state laws, the Living Will and Health Care Proxy may be combined into one document. In such cases, the creator of the document specifies those life-sustaining treatments that are, or are not, to be applied, and then authorizes a proxy to make all other decisions.

Some state legislatures have responded with laws permitting individuals to make advance directives which are written documents evidencing the person's predetermination of the medical treatments they will, and will not, accept under circumstances when they are legally incompetent.

These documents include:
- **Living Wills**
- **Health Care Proxy**

In terms of content, a Health Care Proxy should, as a minimum, include the following:

1. A clear definition of the scope of the proxy's powers or limitations
2. Guidelines for the proxy to follow

Jurisdictional Issues

Some states have enacted laws that recognize the validity of advance directives executed under the laws of other states. Further, it is possible that if the issue came before the U. S. Supreme Court, it would rule that the states had to honor directives created in accordance with each other's laws. The problem, however, is that the issue has not been decided. Consequently, in the face of uncertainty, the prudent course is for concerned individuals to execute an advance directive for each jurisdiction in which they might become hospitalized. In that regard, while it would seem excessive for individuals to create 50 advance directives, it would not be unreasonable to execute one for their home state and any other jurisdiction to which they regularly traveled.

While forms are available from a variety of sources, including national organizations, it should be kept in mind that the validity of these documents is decided under the law of the particular state in which they are executed.

Preparation of Advance Directives

While forms are available from a variety of sources, including national organizations, it should be kept in mind that the validity of these documents is decided under the law of the particular state in which they are executed. In addition, recognizing the personal nature of each individual's views on the subject, it is wise to have such documents custom drafted by a lawyer familiar with the particular individual's values and law of the jurisdiction in question.

Revocable Living Trusts

These documents, more popularly referred to as Living Trusts, have gained interest because of their use as vehicles for avoiding probate costs. In addition, they offer the possibilities of solving the problem of managing an individual's property after they become legally incompetent. While these attributes exist and Revocable Living Trusts are a valuable estate-planning tool, they are not of as broad an applicability as is sometimes assumed. This is because, as will be explained below, there are cases in which any of the three principal goals can be achieved separately, by a simpler, and less costly approach. All things considered, however, the Revocable Living Trust may be preferable over the separate approaches when the client has satisfying more than one goal in mind. It should be noted that these trusts do not offer tax savings. They serve other purposes.

Saving Probate Costs

Regarding probate, the price of having the trust drafted, and the expense of transferring property to it, must be balanced against the potential cost savings. Probate costs may generally be estimated to run from 5% to 10% of the estate, with the largest portion going to legal fees and executor's commissions. In some cases, the client's probate estate will be too small to warrant the expense of setting up a trust. In other situations, the client may not be a suitable candidate for a trust because of the relatively small administrative burden and their personal hesitancy to separate themselves from direct legal title to their property. Consequently, even if they establish such a trust, they may not transfer their property to it. Further, the possibility of really saving legal fees

Revocable Living Trusts are a valuable estate-planning tool, they are not of as broad an applicability as is sometimes assumed. There are cases in which any of the three principal goals — Saving Probate Costs, Estate-Tax Savings, or Managing Assets after Incompetence — can be achieved separately, by a simpler, and less costly approach.

may be small, because the work of handling the assets and the tax issues after the date of death are about the same.

Estate-Tax Savings

In terms of estate-tax savings, a Revocable Living Trust can be used as an alternative to a person's will for purposes of establishing a by-pass trust and marital deduction arrangement. A will is still created in such situations and is referred to as a Pour Over Will. This is because it is used upon the individual's death to direct any remaining probate assets to the hands of the trustee of the Revocable Living Trust. Once in the trustee's hands, the probate assets from the will are combined with the nonprobate assets already in the trust for division into by-pass and marital deduction portions. Keep in mind, however, that the same arrangement of the decedent's assets may be accomplished more simply under a will.

Managing Assets after Incompetence

When an individual creates a Revocable Living Trust, they typically name themselves as the trustee and select an alternate person to act as the trustee if they become unwilling, or unable, to serve during the balance of their life. Consequently, if an individual places their major assets into a Revocable Living Trust, and becomes incompetent, the alternate trustee takes over and manages the property. This saves the family the difficulty and expense of having to get a court-appointed conservator for the incompetent's property. Of course, as previously explained, this same objective could be accomplished more simply, and at less cost, by having the individual execute a Durable Power of Attorney or Springing Durable Power of Attorney.

In terms of estate-tax savings, a Revocable Living Trust can be used as an alternative to a person's will for purposes of establishing a by-pass trust and marital deduction arrangement. A will is still created in such situations and is referred to as a Pour Over Will.

CHAPTER 9

Working With Lawyers

Importance of the Relationship

The purpose of this chapter is to provide information on developing relationships with lawyers, since working with other professionals, and lawyers in particular, is a fundamental element of success in estate planning. In that regard, this chapter will focus on the following three aspects of the matter:

• Networking with lawyers
• Dealing with a prospect's lawyer
• Avoiding problems with the unauthorized practice of law

Establishing Local Networks With Lawyers

Creating a local networking relationship with lawyers can help the agent expand their business into estate-planning, and provide better service to their customers. Specifically, such relationships provide an agent with the following benefits:

• Getting involved and being identified with other professionals reinforces the agent's reputation, position and interest in the estate-planning market.

• Networking is a way for the agent to get local no-cost legal assistance to sharpen and focus estate-planning proposals for specific prospects. In this respect, virtually every top producer I know has a relationship with a local lawyer, whereby they can call the lawyer, free of charge, to ask questions about developing a proposal for a prospect. As will be more fully explained below, the lawyer will take the call because, if the prospect goes for the proposal, it can lead to business for the lawyer.

- A networking relationship with local lawyers can lead to referral business from the lawyer.

From the lawyer's perspective, as indicated above, the relationship with an agent can lead to business for the lawyer. This is because agents are not prohibited from soliciting business the way lawyers are. Consequently, the agent is in a position to act as a catalyst in approaching prospects, and getting them to recognize, and agree to act on, estate-planning problems that may require legal services for which the agent may recommend the lawyer. In addition, the agent can be a resource of information to the lawyer about life insurance products and their uses.

> **The relationship with an agent can lead to business for the lawyer because agents are not prohibited from soliciting business the way lawyers are. The agent is in a position to act as a catalyst in approaching prospects, and getting them to recognize, and agree to act on, estate-planning problems that may require legal services for which the agent may recommend the lawyer.**

What an Agent Should Look for in a Lawyer

The following are the qualities that an agent should seek in selecting a lawyer to establish a relationship with:

- **Quality** — Choose the best, brightest and most professional lawyer that you can associate with. This is because you may be dealing with extremely complicated legal and tax issues, and you want the best legal services for your customers to make sure that matters are handled correctly.

- **Accessibility** — Select a lawyer who will be readily accessible to you (i.e., one who will return your phone calls and is accommodating on short notice).

- **Trust** — Be sure you can trust the lawyer you choose, and feel comfortable with the lawyer's motives and good judgment in dealing with you.

- **Bottom-line conciliator** — Pick a lawyer with a bottom-line view to getting the job done. Choose a conciliator, and facilitator, and do not get involved with a lawyer who is combative or inflexible.

- **Knowledge of the business** — Look for a lawyer who knows, or is willing to learn, about the role of life insurance in estate planning.

- **Belief in the product** — Find a lawyer who believes in life insurance. Avoid lawyers who have negative or ambivalent attitudes toward life insurance. The best indication of a lawyer's views on the subject is the amount of whole-life insurance the lawyer owns. The more permanent life insurance the lawyer owns, the greater the demonstration of his or her belief in the product.

- **Personal compatibility** — Select a lawyer you like as a person. If you cannot develop a personal relationship you will probably not get along professionally either.

- **Primary allegiance** — Do not pick a lawyer who already has a primary allegiance to another agent. Make sure your estate-planning business is the most important.

- **Specialist** — Select a lawyer who specializes in estate planning. The laws pertaining to estate planning are so extensive and complex that a general practitioner is not likely to be an effective resource.

Note that while I have been describing getting involved with one lawyer, I am not suggesting that you should only seek to work with one lawyer. In fact, you should try and develop relationships with as many lawyers as you can deal with effectively. You

I am not suggesting that you should only seek to work with one lawyer. In fact, you should try and develop relationships with as many lawyers as you can deal with effectively.

should also consider working with a firm of several lawyers. Further, seek lawyers who are willing to introduce you to other lawyers.

Finding a Lawyer Who Meets Your Criteria

If you do not know someone in your local area who meets the above criteria, ask other lawyers, CPAs, trust officers and bankers for recommendations. Be sure to interview those who are suggested, and get to know them as much as possible in both business and personal settings. Further, do not hesitate to check the lawyer's credentials with other lawyers in the area.

When contacting a lawyer about establishing a relationship, you should approach the situation as an established professional who is looking for a mutually beneficial relationship, in which you have something to offer.

When contacting a lawyer about establishing a relationship, do not go "hat in hand" as though you are asking the lawyer to do you a favor in agreeing to do business with you. Rather, if you want to be treated with the respect you desire, you should approach the situation as an established professional who is looking for a mutually beneficial relationship, in which you have something to offer. You might begin by inviting a lawyer to breakfast, or lunch, for a meeting at which you may discuss the advantages to both of you in establishing a relationship.

How to Make the Relationship Grow

To successfully deal with professionals, you must also be perceived as a professional, and the first step is acquiring a base of knowledge. This means study through recognized curriculums to receive widely recognized and acknowledged professional designations, such as the CLU, ChFC and CFP. In addition, membership in industry associations, such as The

Society of Financial Service Professionals and The National Association of Estate Planners and Councils is advisable. Further, self-study, industry seminars and agent-study groups are to be pursued. All of these activities will not only provide the knowledge you need, but also give you an identity as a professional, and credibility with those you serve and work with.

In addition, to make your relationship with a lawyer grow, you should also do the following:

- **Regular communication** — You should have regular meetings with the lawyer to talk about estate planning and developing mutual clients. Go prepared, however, to contribute since the lawyer's time is valuable.

- **Keep each other informed** — Each party should seek to keep the other informed of technical and business developments in estate planning that are important to their mutual interest. From the agent's side, the lawyer should be informed about new products and new or unusual uses for existing products in the estate-planning market. The lawyer, on the other hand, should inform the agent about legal/tax developments that are important to estate planning.

- **Give and take** — A successful relationship can only grow if there is open and honest dialog on each other's performance in mutual endeavors.

- **Brainstorming** — The agent and the lawyer should act as brainstorming partners in developing solutions for those they jointly serve.

- **Community image** — Each party should look for ways to help enhance the other's image within the community.

> To successfully deal with professionals, you must also be perceived as a professional, and the first step is acquiring a base of knowledge.

Dealing With a Client's Lawyer

Serving customers in the estate-planning market is, of necessity, a cooperative undertaking because of the diversity and complexity of disciplines involved. Defining roles is, however, the key to successful cooperation with the lawyer, as with other professionals. In that regard, the respective roles of the agent and the lawyer are as follows:

Defining roles is the key to successful cooperation with the lawyer, as with other professionals.

Agent

- Recognize estate-planning-oriented insurance needs and motivate the prospect to take action.
- Provide all the insurance services required.

Lawyer

- Review the agent's proposal for viability considering the legal/tax implications and the prospect's estate-planning objectives.
- Preparation of legal documents.

When to Bring in the Prospect's Lawyer

The prospect's lawyer should generally be brought in immediately after the presentation of the agent's proposal, and the prospect's agreement to take action. This puts the lawyer in a timely position to counsel the prospect on the agent's proposal.

Inquiring About the Prospect's Legal Representation

The agent should always tell the prospect that input from his or her lawyer is welcome. Further, if the prospect does not have a lawyer, and asks for a recommendation, the agent may make such a recommendation, but must be in a position to explain why that lawyer is being recommended.

If the prospect has a lawyer, and the agent decides to recommend a different lawyer, who specializes in the field of estate planning, the agent must tread carefully. In such case, the agent should act by emphasizing the estate-planning qualifications of the specialist, and avoid implying that the prospect's lawyer is not qualified in that area. Further, it should be made clear that the specialist is only being recommended for the specific purpose of implementing the agent's proposal, and no other.

If the prospect prefers to use their own lawyer, for the reason explained below, the agent should ask the prospect if he or she would object to the agent meeting with the lawyer before the prospect does. The agent and the prospect should be aware that the lawyer might send the prospect a bill for the time that the agent spends with the lawyer.

Meeting with the Prospect's Lawyer

The agent should understand that prospects have different levels of involvement with their lawyers. Some consult with their lawyers very little, while others will not make a move without the lawyer's advice. Consequently, before going to see the prospect's lawyer, the agent should try to get a feel for the nature of the relationship between the two.

When meeting the lawyer for the first time, the agent should seek to avoid putting the lawyer on the defensive, by initially assuring the lawyer that the lawyer's input is welcomed by the agent and that nothing will be done until the lawyer agrees that it makes sense.

When preparing an estate-planning proposal to show the lawyer, the agent should base it on as

The agent should understand that prospects have different levels of involvement with their lawyers. Some consult with their lawyers very little, while others will not make a move without the lawyer's advice.

much information as possible from the prospect. The agent should not go to the lawyer looking for information that can be obtained from the prospect. This is because the agent must appear able to help the lawyer serve the prospect, and the possession of key information about the prospect will put the agent in that light, and give the agent credibility with the lawyer. The possession of key personal information that the prospect has given the agent is the best demonstration that the prospect takes the agent seriously. That means the lawyer is going to be more inclined to take the agent and his or her proposal seriously.

The agent must be patient with the lawyer, as lawyers have different degrees of expertise on various subjects. Consequently, the agent must understand that the lawyer may not be very familiar with the subject of the agent's proposal. The agent should, therefore, be prepared to talk technically and present illustrations of what is being proposed for the lawyer's client. It is imperative that, as suggested above, the meeting between the lawyer and the agent take place without the prospect being present. This is because it is a lot easier for the lawyer to admit that he or she is unfamiliar with something when their client is not present. Further, the agent should always present the proposal with a demeanor that shows the proposal is flexible enough to adapt to the lawyer's input.

Avoiding Problems With the Unauthorized Practice of Law

It is appropriate for the agent to recommend the type and amount of life insurance needed for a given estate-planning situation. For example, in an estate-

> **The possession of key personal information that the prospect has given the agent is the best demonstration that the prospect takes the agent seriously. That means the lawyer is going to be more inclined to take the agent and his or her proposal seriously.**

planning case, the agent may gather data regarding the size of the prospect's estate, estimate the tax due under varying assumptions, and project the likely tax and liquidity needs. When it comes, however, to recommending ownership of the insurance, beneficiary designations and settlement options the agent should suggest to the prospect that these issues be discussed with the prospect's lawyer. That is because such issues can have a dramatic impact on the results and consequences of the proposal. Further, with regard to the drafting of legal documents, it is a legal function for the lawyer, and must not be attempted by the agent.

The drafting of legal documents is a legal function for the lawyer, and must not be attempted by the agent.

CHAPTER 10

Developing Relationships With CPAs

The Unique Relationship of CPAs and Their Clients

CPAs tend to have the most frequent contact with their clients. This is because they prepare their client's financial statements and tax returns on a regular basis. Consequently, because of the degree and nature of their contacts with their clients, CPAs are likely to know more about their clients' estate-planning considerations than any of the client's other professional advisors. This also fosters a special relationship of trust and confidence between the CPA and their clients.

CPAs are likely to know more about their clients' estate-planning considerations than any of the client's other professional advisors.

Basis of Cooperation Between Agents and CPAs

Due to their training and knowledge of their client's financial/tax affairs, CPAs are able to both appreciate their client's estate-planning needs for life insurance, and calculate the amounts of coverage required. However, while CPAs are positioned to recognize the need and amount of life insurance warranted in any given situation, they are generally not prepared to deal with the life insurer's underwriting problems.

CPAs are not as knowledgeable as agents on the different kinds of policies, riders, dividend-options, etc., that are required to tailor coverage to a particular client's estate-planning needs.

Further, CPAs are not as knowledgeable as agents on the different kinds of policies, riders, dividend-options, etc., that are required to tailor coverage to a particular client's estate-planning needs.

Creating a Mutually Beneficial Relationship

Historically, agents have viewed CPAs as an excellent source of referred leads, however, changes in the financial services industry are facilitating a mutually beneficial consulting relationship between the two professions. Since CPA firms have clients with insurance needs, that may be more efficiently served through the focus and specialized knowledge of agents, this situation provides the basis for a consulting relationship between CPA firms and agents. Further, since CPAs may be licensed to sell life insurance, they may share commissions with agents on sales to their clients. In that regard, assistance to the CPA in obtaining and maintaining an insurance license will facilitate an ongoing relationship. Finally, to broaden the range of products and services that the agent and CPA can offer to the CPA's estate-planning clients, the CPA should be securities licensed.

CHAPTER 11

Recap & Review:

Questions & Answers to
The Estate Planning Today Handbook

Questions

1. **According to a Cornell University study, the baby boomers will inherit from their parents?**
   a. $8 Trillion   **c.** $20 Billion
   b. $100 Million   **d.** $10 Billion

2. **Since the Economic Growth and Tax Relief Reconciliation Act of 2001 what is the top federal estate and gift tax rate as of 2003?**
   a. 55%   **c.** 70%
   b. 60%   **d.** 49%

3. **An estate-tax return Form 706 is generally due?**
   a. 9 months from the decedent's death
   b. 2 years from the decedents death
   c. 18 months from the date of the decedent's death
   d. 3 years from the decedent's death

4. **In calculating the decedent's "taxable estate" the marital deduction and charitable deduction are subtracted from?**
   a. The adjusted gross estate
   b. The gross estate
   c. The federal estate tax before credits
   d. The net federal estate tax

5. The gift tax is imposed on?
a. The fair-market value of the property when it is given
b. The donor's cost basis for the property
c. The fair-market value of the property when the donor acquired it
d. The fair-market value of the property when the donor dies

6. If a husband and wife "split gifts" they may give a donee?
a. $11,000 each year   c. $22,000 each year
b. $22,000 only once   d. $11,000 each year

7. The gift tax rate is applied to a donor's?
a. Cumulative gifts   c. Gifts from prior years
b. Gifts just for the current year   d. Gifts for future years

8. A "direct skip" is a transfer to a skip person that is?
a. Not subject to estate or gift tax
b. Subject to the estate tax
c. Subject to gift tax
d. Subject to estate or gift tax

9. If a person dies without having executed a "will," they are deemed to have died?
a. Probate   c. Incompetent
b. Intestate   d. Inept

10. To qualify for payment of estate tax in installments under IRC section 6166, the percentage of a decedent's adjusted gross estate comprised of an interest in a farm or other closely held business must be?
a. 35%   c. Less than 35%
b. More than 35%   d. Exactly 35%

11. Leveraging the annual gift-tax exclusion and gift-tax applicable exclusion amount may be accomplished by?
a. Giving property that is expected to appreciate
b. Giving property that is discounted in value

c. Both a and b

d. Neither a or b

12. **If an individual has "incidents of ownership" in a life insurance policy at the time of their death, which of the following will be included in their gross estate?**

    a. All of the death proceeds

    b. None of the death proceeds

    c. The policy's cash value

    d. The policy's fair-market value

13. **If an individual creates a trust with "Crummey Withdrawal Rights," their gifts to the trust will?**

    a. Qualify for the annual exclusion as gifts of a "present interest"

    b. Be disqualified for the annual exclusion

    c. Be included in their gross estate

    d. Be exempt from generation skipping tax

14. **The types of buy and sell agreements are?**

    a. Entity Purchase   **c.** Both a and b

    b. Cross Purchase   **d.** Neither a or b

15. **An IRC section 303 redemption permits a corporation to purchase a portion of a deceased stockholder's shares with the sale taxed to the estate as?**

    a. A capital gain

    b. Dividend

    c. A tax free exchange

    d. A stock option

16. **The first step in the estate-planning process of analysis is to?**

    a. Identify and prioritize the client's objectives

    b. Gather the facts

    c. Match the appropriate estate planning solutions to the client's problems

    d. None of the above

17. **A "durable power of attorney" differs from a power of attorney in that it?**
    a. Does not cease upon the principal's becoming incompetent
    b. Ceases upon the principal's becoming incompetent
    c. Only applies to the principal's real property
    d. Only applies to the principal's personal property

18. **Points to be considered when preparing a "living will" are?**
    a. Artificial nutrition and hydration
    b. Pain-killing drugs
    c. Both a and b
    d. Neither a or b

19. **If a grandparent pays a grandchild's tuition to an educational institution, how are the payments treated?**
    a. Included in the grandparent's estate as incidents of ownership.
    b. Subject to the gift tax
    c. Exempt from the gift tax
    d. Subject to the generation-skipping tax

20. **To avoid the three-year rule of IRC section 2035:**
    a. The insured should purchase and retain ownership of the policy until death
    b. The insured should purchase the policy and give it away after purchase
    c. The policy should be purchased by a third party such as an irrevocable trust
    d. None of the above

Answers

1. **According to a Cornell University study, the baby boomers will inherit from their parents?**
    a. $8 Trillion

2. **Since the Economic Growth and Tax Relief Reconciliation Act of 2001 what is the top federal estate and gift tax rate as of 2003?**
    d. 49%

3. **An estate-tax return Form 706 is generally due?**
    a. 9 months from the decedent's death

4. **In calculating the decedent's "taxable estate" the marital deduction and charitable deduction are subtracted from?**
    a. The adjusted gross estate

5. **The gift tax is imposed on?**
    a. The fair-market value of the property when it is given

6. **If a husband and wife "split gifts" they may give a donee?**
    c. $22,000 each year

7. **The gift tax rate is applied to a donor's?**
    a. Cumulative gifts

8. **A "direct skip" is a transfer to a skip person that is?**
    d. Subject to estate or gift tax

9. **If a person dies without having executed a "will," they are deemed to have died?**
    b. Intestate

10. **To qualify for payment of estate tax in installments under IRC section 6166, the percentage of a decedent's adjusted gross estate comprised of an interest in a farm or other closely held business must be?**
    b. More than 35%

11. **Leveraging the annual gift-tax exclusion and gift-tax applicable exclusion amount may be accomplished by?**
    c. Both a and b

12. **If an individual has "incidents of ownership" in a life insurance policy at the time of their death, which of the following will be included in their gross estate?**
    a. All of the death proceeds

13. **If an individual creates a trust with "Crummey Withdrawal Rights," their gifts to the trust will?**
    a. Qualify for the annual exclusion as gifts of a "present interest"

14. **The types of buy and sell agreements are?**
    c. Both a and b

15. **An IRC section 303 redemption permits a corporation to purchase a portion of a deceased stockholder's shares with the sale taxed to the estate as?**
    a. A capital gain

16. **The first step in the estate-planning process of analysis is to?**
    b. Gather the facts

17. **A "durable power of attorney" differs from a power of attorney in that it?**
    a. Does not cease upon the principal's becoming incompetent

18. **Points to be considered when preparing a "living will" are?**
    c. Both a and b

19. **If a grandparent pays a grandchild's tuition to an educational institution, how are the payments treated?**
    c. Exempt from the gift tax

20. **To avoid the three-year rule of IRC section 2035:**
    c. The policy should be purchased by a third party such as an irrevocable trust

Glossary

Adjusted Gross Estate
A deceased person's gross estate, reduced by funeral and administrative expenses, debts, casualty and theft losses.

Administration of Estate
Involves the collection, management and distribution of a deceased person's estate, including legal proceedings necessary to satisfy claims against the estate.

Administrator/Administratrix
A male or female person appointed by a court to do the administration of an estate.

Applicable Credit Amount
The term given in the Taxpayer Relief Act of 1997 for the unified credit.

Applicable Exclusion Amount
The term given in the Taxpayer Relief Act of 1997 for the exemption equivalent.

Annual Gift-Tax Exclusion
The amount that a person may give each year to as many people as they choose without gift-tax consequences. (For a single individual the amount is $11,000 per recipient. A married couple may give $22,000 per recipient, even though all the property comes from only one of the couple.)

Beneficiary

The person for whom a trust is created or who is named to receive the death proceeds under a life insurance policy.

Bequest

A gift under someone's will of personal property, as opposed to a gift of real estate, sometimes also referred to as a legacy.

Charitable Deduction

A transfer to a charitable organization that is deductible for income-tax purposes and is exempt from gift and estate taxes.

Corpus

The principal of a trust, as opposed to the income.

Credit Estate Tax

A tax imposed by a state to collect the amount allowed as a credit against the federal estate tax that would otherwise be paid to the federal government.

State Death Tax Credit

IRC section 2011 provides a credit against the federal estate tax for estate inheritance legacy or succession taxes paid to any state or the District of Columbia. Pursuant to the 2001 Tax Act, the credit is phased out between 2002 and 2004. Starting in 2005, the credit will be replaced with an unlimited deduction for any of the above taxes paid to any state or the District of Columbia.

Decedent

A deceased person.

Domicile

The place where a person has their permanent home and to which, whenever they are absent, they have the intention of returning. (For example, this is the place where they vote, obtain their drivers license and file their taxes.)

Donee

The person who receives a gift, or is given a power of appointment.

Donor

The person who makes a gift, or grants another person a power of appointment.

Estate Tax

This is a tax imposed on a person's right to transfer property at their death. Estate taxes are imposed by a number of states, as well as the federal government.

Executor/Executrix

An executor is a male, appointed by a deceased person, in their will to administer their estate. An executrix is a female, appointed in a will to administer an estate.

Exemption Equivalent

The amount of property that an individual was permitted to transfer over life, at death, or in combination of both, without incurring federal gift or estate tax. It was termed the applicable exclusion amount under the Taxpayer Relief Act of 1997. Pursuant to the 1997 act, this figure was to increase in stages from $625,000 in 1998 to $1,000,000 by 2006 but it was replaced by the gift-tax applicable exclusion and the estate-tax applicable exclusion pursuant to the 2001 Tax Act.

Fair Market Value

This is the figure at which property is valued for measuring gifts under the gift tax, and for inclusion in the gross estate under the estate tax. It is deemed to be the price at which property would change hands between a willing buyer and a willing seller if both had knowledge of the relevant facts about the property, and neither was under a compulsion to act.

Federal Estate Tax

A federal excise tax that is levied on the right to transfer property at death. It is imposed upon and measured by the fair market value of the property left by the decedent, after the deductions are taken.

Fiduciary

A person who holds a position of trust and must act for another's benefit before their own in the undertaking. (Examples are a trustee or an executor.)

Funded Life Insurance Trust

A trust that holds a life insurance policy, and assets that generate funds to pay premiums.

Future Interest

A right to use or enjoy property in the future.

General Power of Appointment

A power a person holds to direct the disposition of property to anyone, including themselves, their estate or the creditors of their estate. (For example, A creates a trust and gives B a general power of appointment over trust property. This means that B can direct the trustee to give the property to anyone he chooses, including himself, his creditors or the creditors of his estate.)

Generation-Skipping Tax

A federal tax that is imposed on transfers to individuals who are two or more generations below that of the grantor. Its purpose is to prevent the avoidance of tax on a generation through the mechanism of a donor making transfers that skip over the generation in question.

GST Exemption

The amount of property that a person may elect to transfer free of generation-skipping tax, as adjusted for inflation.

Generation-Skipping Tax Trust

A trust that meets the following three requirements: (1) The trust could have a taxable termination or taxable distribution with respect to the transferor. (2) Under the terms of the trust it is unlikely that more than 25% of the trust corpus will be subject to tax in the estate of a non-skip person, such as the transferor's child. (3) The trust is not one of certain types of charitable lead or charitable-remainder trusts.

Gift

A transfer of property for less than a full and adequate consideration.

Gift Splitting

A situation where a husband and wife make a gift to a third party, and elect to treat it, for federal gift-tax purposes, as though it were made one-half by each.

Gift Tax

A tax imposed on transfers of property by gift.

Gift-Tax Applicable Credit

The term given to the credit every individual has against the federal gift tax, pursuant to the 2001 Tax Act. For the years 2004 through 2009 it will be $345,800, and can shelter up to $1 million of taxable gifts from tax. In 2010, the credit will be $330,800, but will still shelter up to $1 million of taxable gifts from tax because the top gift-tax rate will be reduced to 35%.

Gift-Tax Applicable Exclusion

The term given to the amount of property that may be transfered without incurring a federal gift tax. The applicable exclusion for the years 2002 through 2010 is $1 million.

Gift-Tax Marital Deduction

A provision of the federal gift tax that permits certain qualifying gifts to pass between a married couple free of the gift tax. Outright gifts qualify, as well as gifts where the donee spouse has the right to all the income from the property.

Grantor

The individual who establishes a trust and may also be called the settlor.

Gross Estate

The total fair market value of the assets comprising a decedent's estate for federal estate-tax purposes.

Guardian

A individual named in a will or appointed by a court, to take care of the personal matters, property and rights of another individual, who, because of age or disability is incapable of administering their own affairs.

Heir
The person who inherits a decedent's property according state law, when the decedent has died without a will.

Indirect Skip
This term was a creation of the 2001 Tax Act, and refers to any transfer of property to a generation-skipping trust that is not a direct skip and is subject to gift tax.

Inheritance Tax
A tax levied on the right to receive property from a decedent's estate, that is measured by the value of the property passing to the recipient.

Interest
A property right in anything that is less than complete ownership of the property in question.

Inter Vivos Trust
A trust created and taking effect during the grantor's lifetime, as opposed to a testamentary trust that is created in a person's will and does not take effect until the person dies.

Intestate
The situation when a person dies without making a valid will.

Intestate Laws
Individual state laws that provide rules for the distribution of the property of a person who dies intestate (without a valid will).

Irrevocable Trust
A trust that, once created, cannot be altered, revoked or terminated by the grantor.

Joint Tenancy With Right of Survivorship

The ownership of property by two or more persons in such a manner that upon the death of a person, the survivor or survivors obtain the deceased person's ownership interest.

Legacy

A disposition of personal property under a person's will also referred to as a bequest.

Legatee

A person who receives a legacy (personal property) under a will.

Life Insurance Trust

A trust holding life insurance policies and possibly other assets.

Life Estate

A right to enjoy property for a period measured by the duration of the life of the person holding it, or the duration of some other person's life.

Limited Power of Appointment

A power given to a person that allows them to direct that property be given to another person, but not themselves.

Marital Deduction Trust

A trust that holds property for a surviving spouse that qualifies for the marital deduction.

Non-Probate Property

Property that does not pass under the will or intestate laws, and is not subject to estate administration. Typical examples are life insurance benefits paid to a named beneficiary, property passing to a joint tenant by survivorship, and qualified pension benefits paid to a named beneficiary.

Power of Appointment
A right given to another person or reserved by a person for themselves, to direct the disposition of property subject to the limits that the donor of the power prescribes.

Present Interest
A right to presently use or enjoy property.

Principal
The property comprising an estate or trust that is sometimes referred to as the corpus.

Probate
The process of having a will officially recognized by a court.

Probate Property
Property that passes under a person's will.

Remainder Interest
An interest in property that takes effect after the termination of a prior interest. (For example, if A has the right to all of the income from a trust for A's life, and after A's death, B has the right to the trust corpus, B has a remainder interest.)

Residuary Estate
This is the part of an individual's estate that is left after the payment of debts, expenses and taxes, and the distribution of amounts of cash or property to estate beneficiaries who are named to receive such specific distributions, that are called legacies or bequests. The balance of the estate, in the form of the residuary, is then distributed according to a clause in the will

that usually exists covering the disposition of property not specifically allocated to particular beneficiaries.

Reversionary Interest

The right to receive back the use or enjoyment of property that an individual has transferred to, or for, the benefit of another person, after that other person's interest has terminated. (For example, where A creates a trust providing B a life-income interest, with the property to revert to A upon B's death, A has a reversionary interest.)

Revocable Trust

A trust that the grantor can revoke, or terminate, and receive back the corpus.

Sprinkling or Spray Trust

A trust under which the trustee has the discretionary power to accumulate or pay income to the beneficiaries in equal or unequal shares.

Taxable Estate

The gross estate, less allowable deductions, debts, taxes and administrative expenses.

Tennancy by the Entirety

Property held by a husband and wife in a form that neither one can dispose of their interest during the life of the other without the other's consent. Further, on the death of one spouse, the entire ownership interest belongs to the survivor.

Tennancy in Common

A form of undivided joint ownership by two or more persons under which, upon the death of a joint owner, that person's interest passes as a part of their estate.

Testamentary

A disposition of property by a person's will.

Testamentary Trust

A trust created under a person's will and taking no effect until their death and the will being probated.

Testate

A term that describes a situation when a person has died and left a will.

Testator

A person who has died with a will.

Trust

An arrangement under which one party, acting as a fiduciary, holds legal title to property that they must manage for the benefit of another party.

Trustee

The holder of legal title to property that must be managed in a fiduciary manner for the benefit of another party.

Unified Credit

A credit that every individual had against the federal gift and estate taxes. It was the same as the exemption equivalent. Pursuant to the Taxpayer Relief Act of 1997, the term for this tax credit was changed to the Applicable Credit Amount and it was to increase in stages from $202,050, in 1998, to $345,800, by 2006. Pursuant to the 2001 Tax Act, the applicable credit amount was divided into the gift-tax applicable credit amount and the estate-tax applicable credit in 2002.

Resource Guide
Tools for Success

Recommended Reading

The Long-Term Care Planning Guide:
Practical Steps for Making Difficult Decisions

By Don Korn

This compact, new guide, walks you through the maze of issues you need to consider when making long-term care choices. In his simple, straightforward style, financial-planning expert Don Korn focuses on the most common and crucial factors for determining long-term care needs.

$19.95   Item #T183X-820537

Understanding Erisa:
A Compact Guide to the Landmark Act

By Ken Ziesenheim

This new guide clarifies the basic principles of ERISA — and the liabilities to which fiduciaries may be subjected — in simple, understandable terms. Perfect for establishing procedures within your practice, and for ensuring everyone in your organization is in compliance.

$19.95   Item #T183X-48535

Estate Planning, 6th edition

By Dearborn Financial Publishing

The purpose of this course is to equip the financial-services professional with the technical knowledge necessary to operate on a professional level. The knowledge of estate planning offered in this course will increase opportunities to render a valuable service to clients and, at the same time, present a means of increasing personal stature through individual achievement.

$50.00   Item #T183X-49217

J.K. Lasser's New Rules for Estate and Tax Planning

By Harold Apolinsky and Stewart Welch

The Economic Growth and Tax Relief Reconciliation Act of 2001 will affect numerous aspects of your financial life — none more important than how you plan your estate. This new tax law includes the first major estate-tax revision in over twenty years. Use *J.K. Lasser's New Rules for Estate and Tax Planning* to learn how the rules have changed and what you can do now to effectively plan your estate.

$16.95   Item #T183X-48674

The Complete Guide to Compensation Planning with Life Insurance

By Louis S. Shuntich, J.D., LL.M.

Help your clients attract and retain high caliber employees with this new, compact reference guide. The Society of Financial Professionals has teamed up with tax and compensation planning expert, Lou Shuntich, to bring it all together in one compact volume.

$29.95   Item #T183X-1611782

The Life Insurance Handbook

By Louis S. Shuntich, J.D., LL.M.

Term life insurance. Whole life. Variable and Universal life insurance. As the list of choices for insurance products continues to grow, The Life Insurance Handbook is the perfect learning too for keeping busy financial professionals and their clients up-to-date.

$19.95   Item #T183X-64203

These books along with hundreds of others are available at a discount from FP Books. To place an order or find out more,
Call 1-800-511-5667 ext. 183 *or visit our web site at*

www.fpbooks.com

Important Internet Sites

www.nafep.com

The National Association of Financial & Estate Planning
(NAFEP) has developed an array of both standard and sophisticated estate planning programs which Associates provide to their clients. The organization provides significant education, support and materials to the Associates. This support gives Associates a great range of information and tools to help clients with estate planning.

www.insuranceplanningadvisors.com

Halloran Financial Services, specialists in estate and financial planning, providing comprehensive solutions for insurance and long-term care needs for over 20 years. For information contact: **Halloran Financial Services**
Mike@insuranceplanningadvisors.com
(781) 449-4556
400 Hillside Ave, Needham, MA 02494

www.financialpro.org

For more than 70 years, the **Society of Financial Service Professionals** — formerly the American Society of CLU & ChFC — has been helping individuals, families, and businesses achieve financial security. Society members can provide consumers expert assistance with: estate, retirement and financial planning; employee benefits; business and compensation planning; and life, health, disability, and long-term care insurance.

www.fpanet.org

The Financial Planning Association is the membership organization for the financial planning community. FPA has been built around four Core Values — Competence, Integrity, Relationships and Stewardship. We want as members those who share our Core Values. FPA's primary aim is to be the community that fosters the value of financial planning and advances the financial planning profession.

www.fpbooks.com

FP Books, a division of SuperBookDeals, is the #1 source for financial planning and investment books, videos, software, and other related products. Find the most thorough selection of new releases and hard to find titles geared towards financial planners and advisors.

www.iarfc.org

The **IARFC** is the fastest growing organization in financial services, increasing nearly 3% per month — now over 2,600 professional members. Prospects and clients expect that their financial advisors to maintain meaningful professional standards. There are seven hallmarks: education, examination, ethics, experience, licensing, continued conduct and continuing education.

▲ ▲ ▲ ▲ ▲ ▲

Publications of Interest

E-Alert
Thornburg Investment Management
www.thornburginvestments.com/

Kiplinger's Retirement Report
www.kiplinger.com/retreport/

Barron's Online
www.barrons.com

The Wall Street Journal Online
http://online.wsj.com/public/us

FREE CATALOG

Innovative Products for Successful Financial Planners at Everyday Low Prices!

Browse over *5,000 titles* ranging from subjects such as...

- Financial Advising & Practice Management
- Marketing Your Services
- Asset Allocation & Portfolio Management
- Insurance, Retirement & Estate Planning
- General Investing
- Client & Premium Giveaways - and More!

SAVE **15%**
ask for ext. T183

Call NOW for a FREE Catalog!
1-800-511-5667 ext. T183
410-964-0026 - or go to
www.fpbooks.com

TRUST

It's a necessity,
not an indulgence,
in the investor-adviser
relationship.

Clients TRUST their
financial advisers to understand
the real goals that drive them.
But increased competition,
a continuously evolving industry
and unrelenting demands
are making it more difficult
to grow professionally and
guide your clients.

**Society of
Financial Service Professionals®**

Align yourself with a professional organization that can support your success. The Society of Financial Service Professionals offers:

A choice of nine
Professional Interest Sections

Comprehensive and up-to-date
continuing education

High quality networking opportunities

Client referral, acquisition and
retention tools

Discounts on practice-building
products and services

**Society members provide services
in the following areas:**

- Financial Planning
- Life, Health & Disability Insurance
- Investment Management
- Mutual Funds and Securities
- Retirement Counseling & Planning
- Long-term Care and Eldercare Counseling
- Estate Planning
- Business & Compensation Planning
- Employee Benefits/Group Insurance
- Liability Risk Management
- Tax Planning & Counseling

To learn more call
800-392-6900
or visit
www.financialpro.org

**Society of Financial Service Professionals
270 S. Bryn Mawr Avenue
Bryn Mawr, PA 19010-2195**

Solutions for a Secure Future™

Free 2 Week Trial Offer for U.S. Residents From Investor's Business Daily:

INVESTOR'S BUSINESS DAILY will provide you with the facts, figures, and objective news analysis you need to succeed.

Investor's Business Daily is formatted for a quick and concise read to help you make informed and profitable decisions.

To take advantage of this free 2 week trial offer, e-mail us at customerservice@fpbooks.com or visit our website at www.fpbooks.com where you find other free offers as well.

You can also reach us by calling 1-800-511-5667 or fax us at 410-964-0027.

About the Author

Louis S. Shuntich is a consultant and author who has served in the Law Department of a major life insurance company for 26 years, where he specialized in business insurance and estate planning. He received his B.S. cum laude from Rider University, his J.D. from The College of William and Mary and his LLM (in Taxation) from New York University.

He is an assistant editor of the *Journal of Financial Service Professionals*, a member of the Association for Advanced Life Underwriting Business Insurance and Estate Planning Committee, was chairman of the American Council of Life Insurance Split-Dollar Task Force and has served on the Life Underwriter Training Council's Content and Techniques Committee. He is a member of the Speakers Bureau of the Society of Financial Service Professionals and the Speakers Bureau of the National Association of Estate Planners and Councils. He has also appeared on the CNBC Power Lunch and Health and Lifestyles programs answering questions about retirement and estate planning.

This book, along with other books, are available at discounts

that make it realistic to provide them as gifts to your customers, clients, and staff. For more information on these long-lasting, cost-effective premiums, please call John Boyer at 800-272-2855 or e-mail him at john@traderslibrary.com